HOW
Happiness
Happens

FINDING LASTING JOY IN A WORLD OF COMPARISON, DISAPPOINTMENT, AND UNMET EXPECTATIONS

STUDY GUIDE | SIX SESSIONS

MAX LUCADO

WITH ANDREA LUCADO

THOMAS NELSON
Since 1798

Published in Nashville, Tennessee, by Thomas Nelson. Thomas Nelson is a registered trademark of HarperCollins Christian Publishing, Inc.

Published in association with Anvil II Management, Inc.

All Scripture quotations, unless otherwise noted, are taken from the Holy Bible, New International Version®. NIV®. Copyright 1973, 1978, 1984, 2011 by Biblica, Inc.® Used by permission. All rights reserved worldwide.

Scripture quotations marked ESV are taken from The ESV® Bible (The Holy Bible, English Standard Version®). ESV® Text Edition: 2016. Copyright © 2001 by Crossway, a publishing ministry of Good News Publishers.

Scripture quotations marked MSG are taken from The Message, copyright © 1993, 2002, 2018 by Eugene H. Peterson. Used by permission of NavPress. All rights reserved. Represented by Tyndale House Publishers, Inc.

Scripture quotations marked NASB are taken from the New American Standard Bible®, Copyright © 1960, 1962, 1963, 1968, 1971, 1972, 1973, 1975, 1977, 1995 by The Lockman Foundation. Used by permission.

Scripture quotations marked NCV are taken from the New Century Version®. Copyright © 2005 by Thomas Nelson. Used by permission. All rights reserved.

Scripture quotations marked NKJV taken from the New King James Version®. Copyright © 1982 by Thomas Nelson. Used by permission. All rights reserved.

Scripture quotations marked NLT are taken from the Holy Bible, New Living Translation, copyright © 1996, 2004, 2015 by Tyndale House Foundation. Used by permission of Tyndale House Publishers, Inc., Carol Stream, Illinois 60188. All rights reserved.

Scripture quotations marked NRSV are taken from the New Revised Standard Version Bible, copyright © 1989 the Division of Christian Education of the National Council of the Churches of Christ in the United States of America. Used by permission. All rights reserved.

Scripture quotations marked VCE are taken from The Voice™. Copyright © 2008 by Ecclesia Bible Society. Used by permission. All rights reserved.

Thomas Nelson titles may be purchased in bulk for educational, business, fundraising, or sales promotional use. For information, please email SpecialMarkets@ThomasNelson.com.

ISBN 978-0-310-10571-8

First Printing August 2019 / Printed in the United States of America

Contents

A Word from Max Lucado

Happiness. Everyone craves it, wants it, searches for it. We are longing for this sense of contentment and well-being. Worldwide, people profess that happiness is their most cherished goal.[1] The most popular class in the three-century history of Yale University is on happiness.[2]

We think we've figured happiness out. We think we know how and where to find it. The often-used front door to happiness is the one described by the advertising companies: *acquire, retire,* and *aspire* to drive faster, dress trendier, and drink more. Happiness happens when you lose the weight, get the date, find the mate, or discover your fate. It's wide, this front door to happiness . . . or so they claim.

Advertising companies claim to have the key to happiness, yet our society still seems to be struggling to find it. Only one-third of Americans surveyed said they were happy. In the nine-year history of the Harris Poll Survey of American Happiness, the highest index was only 35 percent. This means a cloud of perpetual grayness overshadows two out of three people.[3]

What's up? How do we explain the gloom? While the answers are varied and complex, among them must be this idea: *we are using the wrong door.*

The motto on the front door says, "Happiness happens when you *get*." The sign on the lesser-used back door counters, "Happiness happens when you *give*." And standing at the entryway to welcome you is Jesus of Nazareth.

Jesus was accused of much, but he was never, ever described as a grump, sourpuss, or self-centered jerk. People didn't groan when he appeared. They didn't duck for cover when he entered the room.

He called them by name.

He listened to their stories.

He answered their questions.

His purpose statement read, "I came to give life with joy and abundance" (John 10:10 VCE). Jesus was happy, and he wants us to be the same.

But how? How do we attain this type of true side-door happiness? We can begin by taking a cue from the New Testament. The New Testament contains more than fifty "one another" statements—practical principles for making happiness happen. In this study, I have condensed them down into a list of six:

1. Accept one another (Romans 15:7)
2. Bear with one another (Ephesians 4:2)
3. Serve one another (Galatians 5:13)
4. Forgive one another (Ephesians 4:32)
5. Carry one another's burdens (Galatians 6:2)
6. Love one another (1 John 3:11)

This is how we give happiness away and, in turn, get happiness ourselves. So let's open the door to each of these "one another" passages and embark on a happiness project.

How to Use This Guide

Looking for greater happiness in your life? Then you are in the right place. The *How Happiness Happens Video Study* is designed to be experienced in a group setting such as a Bible study, Sunday school class, or any small group gathering. Each session begins with a brief reflection and "Talk About It" questions to get you and your group thinking about the topic. You will then watch a video with Max Lucado and jump into some directed small-group discussion. You will finish each session with a brief closing activity and prayer as a group.

Each person in the group should have his or her own study guide, which includes video teaching notes, Bible study and group discussion questions, and between-sessions personal studies to help you reflect and apply the material to your life during the week. You are also encouraged to have a copy of the *How Happiness Happens* book, as reading the book alongside the curriculum will provide you with deeper insights and make the journey more meaningful. See the "For Next Week" section at the end of each session for the chapters in the book that correspond to material you and your group are discussing.

To get the most out of your group experience, keep the following points in mind. First, the real growth in this study will happen during your small-group time. This is where you will process the content of Max's message (and the testimonies), ask questions, and learn from others as you hear what God is doing in their lives.

For this reason, it is important for you to be fully committed to the group and attend each session so that you can build trust and rapport with the other members. If you choose to only "go through the motions," or if you refrain from participating, there is a lesser chance you will find what you're looking for during this study.

Second, remember the goal of your small group is to serve as a place where people can share, learn about God, and build intimacy and friendship. For this reason, seek to make your group a "safe place." This means being honest about your thoughts and feelings and listening carefully to everyone else's opinion. (*Note: If you are a group leader, there are additional instructions and resources in the back of the book for leading a productive discussion group.*)

Third, resist the temptation to "fix" a problem someone might be having or to correct his or her theology, as that's not the purpose of your small-group time. Also, keep everything your group shares confidential. This will foster a rewarding sense of community in your group and create a place where people can heal, be challenged, and grow spiritually.

Following your group time, maximize the impact of the course with the additional between-session studies. For each session, you may wish to complete the personal study all in one sitting or spread it out over a few days (for example, working on it a half hour a day on four different days that week).

Note that if you are unable to finish (or even start!) your between-sessions personal study, you should still attend the group study video session. You are still wanted and welcome at the group even if you don't have your "homework" done.

Keep in mind the videos, discussions, and activities are simply meant to kick-start your imagination so you are open to both what God wants you to hear and how to apply it to your life. As you go through this study, be watching for what God is saying as it relates to each of the "one another" passages you will be studying: *accepting* one another, *bearing* with one another, *serving* one another, *forgiving* one another, *carrying* one another's burdens, and, finally, *loving* one another as Jesus loves you.

As you open the door to each of these "one another" passages and embark on your own personal happiness project, you will discover what the Bible teaches and research affirms: "It is more blessed to give than to receive" (Acts 20:35).

Session One

Accept One Another

*It's hard to know the best way to respond to people who
represent your "opposite you." Do you ignore them? Leave the
room when they enter so you don't say something you later
will regret? Share a meal and discuss your differences?
Dismiss your differences? How do you find and show
acceptance toward someone when you would rather show
them the door? The answer can be found in this admonition:
"Accept one another, then, just as Christ accepted you, in order
to bring praise to God" (Romans 15:7).*

MAX LUCADO

Opening Reflection

We are creatures of comfort and creatures of habit. We like the familiar and predictable. We like agreement over conflict. Peace over disruption. These are the things that make us feel happy, content, at rest. And all these things—comfort, familiarity, agreement—are achievable as long as we interact only with people who are just like us. People who are part of the same political party, church denomination, ethnic group, or country. People who like what we like and dislike what we dislike.

This is all fine and good, but there is one problem. To live in the world we live in today, we are bound to interact with someone who is different from us. A coworker, someone next to us on the bus, a neighbor, classmate, teacher, or pastor. We have been created equal, but we have not been created alike. For this reason, if our happiness depends on being surrounded by people who agree with us all the time, we won't feel happy very often.

In this week's study, we will be looking at Romans 15:7, where Paul wrote, "Accept one another, then, just as Christ accepted you, in order to bring praise to God." Note that Paul did not specify to the Roman church *whom* they should accept. He did not say *accept the people you like* or *accept the people who look like you* or *accept the people who think the same way as you think.* He left it general and open-ended. Accept whom? One another.

Could it be we are called to accept the Democrat and the Republican? The Midwesterner and Southerner? The immigrant and the native? The Catholic and the Protestant?

Further, Paul instructs us to accept one another as Christ accepted us. How did Christ accept us? He loved us so much that he made the greatest sacrifice for us. He died for us. Rose from the grave for us. Left the Holy Spirit to dwell within us. Christ welcomed us into the family of God. And this, the Bible says, is how we are to welcome others.

So open your mind and your heart as you explore today's topic. Discover how accepting one another can make happiness happen in your own life—and for those you accept as Christ accepted you.

Talk About It

If you or any of your group members are just getting to know one another, take a few minutes to introduce yourselves. Then, to kick things off, discuss one of the following questions:

- What is something that made you happy this week?

—or—

- What comes to mind when you think of "accepting one another"?

13

Hearing the Word

Invite someone to read aloud Romans 15:5–7. Listen for fresh insights as you hear the verses being read, and then discuss the questions that follow.

> [5] May the God who gives endurance and encouragement give you the same attitude of mind toward each other that Christ Jesus had, [6] so that with one mind and one voice you may glorify the God and Father of our Lord Jesus Christ. [7] Accept one another, then, just as Christ accepted you, in order to bring praise to God.

What is one key insight that stands out to you from this passage?

In what ways did that represent a new insight?

According to this passage, why should we accept one another?

Video Teaching Notes

Play the video segment for session one. As you watch, use the following outline to record any thoughts or concepts that stand out to you.

Happiness happens when you choose to give it away. Jesus' words were spot-on when he said, "It is more blessed to give than to receive" (Acts 20:35).

One of the most difficult relationship questions is what to do with your "opposite you." You know the one—it's the person with whom you fundamentally disagree.

Accept one another. The verb Paul uses for *accept* means more than to merely tolerate or coexist with someone. It means to welcome the person into your fellowship.

While Jesus doesn't accept our sinful behavior, he always accepts us as his wayward children. He doesn't tell us to clean up before we can come to him.

You are never called to redeem the world. Happiness happens not by *fixing* people but by *accepting* them and entrusting them to God's care.

It is one thing to have an opinion. It's something else to have a fight. So when you sense the volume increasing and the heat rising, close your mouth.

Happiness happens when you show other people that they matter. The Bible says that as you greet others and show acceptance, you *demonstrate* the love of Christ.

Three phrases—"I love you," "I forgive you," "supper's ready"— summarize Jesus' message. He came with love, grace . . . and a dinner invitation.

I got to the point where I realized that if there was going to be joy in my life, I had to be a joyful person. So I bought a bunch of candy, and I went around the office and gave it out. I walked past a conference room and I saw a coworker that I wasn't particularly fond of, and I thought, "Maybe he needs some joy." So I placed some candy on the table. He looked at me and he said, "Is this a joke?" We both got a chuckle— it was a nice moment for both of us to just let our guards down and be kind to each other. It's not like this was an earth-shattering experience that changed either of us. But I think it was impactful for the both of us to just have something that brought a little kindness, a little happiness, to both of our lives.

— ALLISON, FROM THE VIDEO

Group Discussion

Take a few minutes with your group members to discuss what you just watched and explore these concepts in Scripture.

1. Jesus said, "It is more blessed to give than to receive" (Acts 20:35). Have you ever experienced happiness by giving it away? If so, describe that experience.

2. Paul instructs, "Accept one another, then, just as Christ accepted you" (Romans 15:7). What is the difference between *accepting* someone and *tolerating* someone?

3. Whom would you consider your "opposite you"? (This could be someone from your past or someone in your life today.) How do you typically interact with that person?

4. Read John 1:14. What does it mean to be full of both *grace* and *truth*? Who is someone in your life who is full of grace and truth? How does this person show these qualities?

5. Read Romans 14:1–3. Social media provides a hostile environment where people often argue, disagree with each other, and tear each other down. How can this passage be applied to the way we get into arguments and debates on social media and elsewhere?

6. Read Romans 16:16. Why do you think Paul made it a point to instruct the church members in Rome to greet one another?

7. When was a time someone greeted you when you were having a bad day or going through a difficult season? How did that greeting make you feel?

8. What part of Allison's story resonated with you? After listening to her story, did anyone come to mind whom you need to accept? How could you work to accept this person?

Closing Activity

To apply today's study, complete the Scripture exercise below:

- *Fill in the blank with the name of someone who is difficult for you to accept:* "Accept _____, then, just as Christ accepted you, in order to bring praise to God" (Romans 15:7).

- *Fill in the blank with the name of someone with whom you often disagree:* "Be in agreement, understanding

_____, loving each other as family, being kind and humble" (1 Peter 3:8 NCV).

- *Fill in the blanks with the name of someone you need to greet and how you could greet him or her* (for example, a handshake, a "hello," a note of encouragement): "Greet _____ with a holy _____" (Romans 16:16).

If you feel comfortable, share with your group what this experience was like for you.

Closing Prayer

Close your time by spending time with your heavenly Father. Using the prompts below, have one person lead your group in a time of group prayer:

- Thank God for accepting you into his family by giving you his Son, Jesus.
- Confess that you have not always been accepting of others in the past.
- Ask God to give you empathy to help you better understand the people around you.
- Praise God for creating such a diverse world full of beauty and creativity.

Between-Sessions
Personal Study

Session One

Reflect on the material you've covered this week in *How Happiness Happens* by engaging in any or all of the following between-sessions activities. Each personal study consists of four days of reflection activities to help you implement what you learned in the group time. The time you invest will be well spent, so let God use it to draw you closer to him. At your next meeting, share any key points or insights that stood out to you as you spent this time with the Lord.

Accepting Others

During your group time you discussed Romans 15:5–7, where Paul instructed you to "accept one another, then, just as Christ accepted you, in order to bring praise to God." In today's lesson, you will dig deeper into this passage in order to better understand why and how you can accept others in the way that Christ accepts you. Begin by rereading Romans 15:5–7:

⁵ May the God who gives endurance and encouragement give you the same attitude of mind toward each
other that Christ Jesus had, ⁶ so that with one mind
and one voice you may glorify the God and Father of
our Lord Jesus Christ. ⁷ Accept one another, then, just
as Christ accepted you, in order to bring praise to God.

1. According to Paul, what does God give us? How has he
   given you these things?

2. What do you think Paul meant when he wrote we are to
   have "the same attitude of mind toward each other that
   Christ Jesus had" (verse 5)?

3. Paul describes this "attitude of mind" in Philippians 2:5–8:

   ⁵ In your relationships with one another, have the
   same mindset as Christ Jesus: ⁶ who, being in very
   nature God, did not consider equality with God
   something to be used to his own advantage; ⁷ rather,
   he made himself nothing by taking the very nature
   of a servant, being made in human likeness. ⁸ And
   being found in appearance as a man, he humbled
   himself by becoming obedient to death—even death
   on a cross!

According to this passage, what was Christ's mindset?

4. How can you mimic this mindset toward others? How could this mindset help you to better accept others—even those difficult people in your life?

5. According to Romans 15:6, how does unity with one another bring glory to God?

6. How could disunity hurt the image of God, Christ, and the church?

7. Have you ever experienced disunity in the church? If so, what was that experience like?

8. How have your experiences with other believers shaped the way you view God, Jesus, and the body of Christ?

9. Have you ever been a part of a faith community that felt unified? How did being a part of a unified body affect your faith?

10. Perhaps you have never attended church because of the disunity you've observed. It may not seem like a welcoming place for you. Have you had any new observations about Jesus or the church after today's study on acceptance and unity? Explain.

Prayer: *Ask God to give you the mind of Christ. Ask for humility. Ask for love for one another and a desire for unity. Repent of any moments this week when you may have contributed to disunity either in the church, in your home, or in your workplace. Ask God to give you opportunities to work toward unity and, therefore, to glorify him.*

Practicing Empathy

Empathy is the practice of putting yourself in someone else's shoes. When you empathize with others, you are able to accept them, even if they have different beliefs, come from a different culture, or have a different socioeconomic background. Begin today's study by reading through the story of Levi, who would later be called Matthew:

[27] Jesus went out and saw a tax collector named Levi sitting in the tax collector's booth. Jesus said to him, "Follow me!" [28] So Levi got up, left everything, and followed him.

[29] Then Levi gave a big dinner for Jesus at his house. Many tax collectors and other people were eating there, too. [30] But the Pharisees and the men who taught the law for the Pharisees began to complain to Jesus' followers, "Why do you eat and drink with tax collectors and sinners?"

[31] Jesus answered them, "It is not the healthy people who need a doctor, but the sick. [32] I have not come to invite good people but sinners to change their hearts and lives" (Luke 5:27–32 NCV).

Although Levi was a Jew, tax collectors were not well liked by other Jews. They considered Levi a "sellout"—someone who worked for the Roman government and got to keep a cut of the taxes he took from others.[4] So though Levi was rich in money, he wasn't rich in character or reputation. Taking this into consideration, put yourself in the shoes of the different characters in this story and answer the following questions.

Jesus

1. Why do you think Jesus wanted Levi to be his follower even though Levi had a bad reputation?

2. How do you think Jesus felt at the dinner at Levi's house? Celebratory, relaxed, or perhaps nervous to be around this type of crowd? Explain your response.

3. Why do you think Jesus reacted to the Pharisees the way he did (see verses 31–32)?

Levi

4. How do you think Levi felt when Jesus looked at him and said, "Follow me"?

5. What do you think Levi was thinking when the Pharisees walked into the party?

The Pharisees

6. Why do you think the Pharisees judged Jesus for hanging out with tax collectors?

7. What do you think the Pharisees thought about Jesus' reply, "I have not come to invite good people but sinners to change their hearts and lives"?

8. Which character in the story do you identify with the most—Jesus, Levi, or the Pharisees? Why?

9. How did considering three different points of view help you understand this story better or change your interpretation of the story?

10. Is there anyone in your life you need to empathize with? Maybe someone you don't get along with or have had an argument with recently? How could you put yourself in that person's shoes today?

Prayer: *Thank God for sending Jesus to serve as an example for how you should accept and empathize with others. Ask God to help you empathize with those people who are often difficult to handle. Ask God to give you a new understanding of those individuals.*

Accepting Yourself

If you are finding it difficult to accept others, it could be because you haven't accepted yourself. The Bible says that in Christ we are a new creation (see 2 Corinthians 5:17). We have received the spirit of adoption and have been adopted into God's own family (see Romans 8:15). Because of this, we can be confident that we are fully loved and accepted by God and nothing can separate us from that love (see Romans 8:38–39). With this in mind, spend some time today looking at what the Bible has to say about your acceptance into Christ's family and how believing in that fact could help you accept others. Begin by reading Romans 5:8–10:

> 8 But God demonstrates His own love toward us, in that while we were still sinners, Christ died for us. 9 Much more then, having now been justified by His blood, we shall be saved from wrath through Him. 10 For if when we were enemies we were reconciled to God through the death of His Son, much more, having been reconciled, we shall be saved by His life (NKJV).

1. How did God demonstrate his love for you?

2. What did Christ's death on the cross do to your relationship with God?

3. How does this passage help you to understand your acceptance by God through Christ?

4. Read the following story of Jesus and the Samaritan woman told in John 4:

> [3] [Jesus] left Judea and departed again to Galilee.
> [4] But He needed to go through Samaria.
> [5] So He came to a city of Samaria which is called Sychar, near the plot of ground that Jacob gave to his son Joseph. [6] Now Jacob's well was there. Jesus therefore, being wearied from His journey, sat thus by the well. It was about the sixth hour.
> [7] A woman of Samaria came to draw water. Jesus said to her, "Give Me a drink." [8] For His disciples had gone away into the city to buy food.
> [9] Then the woman of Samaria said to Him, "How is it that You, being a Jew, ask a drink from me, a Samaritan woman?" For Jews have no dealings with Samaritans.
> [10] Jesus answered and said to her, "If you knew the gift of God, and who it is who says to you, 'Give Me a drink,' you would have asked Him, and He would have given you living water."
> [11] The woman said to Him, "Sir, You have nothing to draw with, and the well is deep. Where then do You get that living water? . . ."

¹³ Jesus answered and said to her, "Whoever drinks of this water will thirst again, ¹⁴ but whoever drinks of the water that I shall give him will never thirst. . . ."

¹⁵ The woman said to Him, "Sir, give me this water, that I may not thirst, nor come here to draw."

¹⁶ Jesus said to her, "Go, call your husband, and come here."

¹⁷ The woman answered and said, "I have no husband."

Jesus said to her, "You have well said, 'I have no husband,' ¹⁸ for you have had five husbands, and the one whom you now have is not your husband; in that you spoke truly."

¹⁹ The woman said to Him, "Sir, I perceive that You are a prophet. . . . ²⁵ I know that Messiah is coming" (who is called Christ). "When He comes, He will tell us all things."

²⁶ Jesus said to her, "I who speak to you am He" (verses 3–11, 13–19, 25–26 NKJV).

What kind of person was the woman in this story? What status do you think she held in society?

5. Who initiated this conversation—the woman or Jesus? Why is this significant?

6. According to verse 9, how did the woman feel about Jesus' request?

7. Jesus breaks three cultural barriers during this conversation. First, he speaks to a woman—and traditionally, Jewish men were not to be seen conversing with women.[5] Second, he speaks with a Samaritan, and as the passage says, Jews had no dealings with Samaritans at the time (see verse 9). Third, he speaks to a woman who he knows has had more than one husband and is now with a man she isn't married to (see verses 17–18). Considering this, why do you think Jesus still spoke with the woman?

8. What does Jesus do in verse 26? Jesus was not yet telling everyone who he was at this point in his ministry, so why do you think he chose to reveal himself to this woman?

9. What does this story tell you about the type of people Jesus does and does not accept? What does this story tell you about how Jesus accepts *you*?

_10._ Think about the Samaritan woman in this story. If Jesus fully accepted her, what does this mean about his acceptance of you—faults and all?

Prayer: _If you've never accepted God's love, pray about that now. Ask God to show you the fullness of his love and acceptance toward you. If you have accepted the love of God through Christ, then spend some time thanking God for sending his Son, Jesus. Ask him what areas of your life you might be holding on to or hiding because you don't think they are worthy of his love. Ask God to help you feel his love for your full self, not just the "good" parts._

Further Reflection

Reflect on what you studied this week: acceptance of others, empathy, and self-acceptance. Journal your thoughts or write them as a prayer to God, whether you need to ask him questions about what you learned, thank him for what you have learned, or ask him what to do next now that you have a better understanding of these topics in Scripture. Also write down any observations or questions that you want to bring to your next group time.

For Next Week: In preparation for next week, read chapters 2–3 in _How Happiness Happens._

Session Two

Bear with One Another

*Pet peeves. "He gets under my skin." "She gets on
my nerves." "He is such a pain in my neck." These phrases
about our pet peeves reveal who actually suffers.
Whose skin? Whose nerves? Whose neck? Ours!
Every pet peeve writes a check on our joy account. How can
we help people smile if our happiness account is overdrawn?
We can't. For this reason, the apostle Paul said, "Be patient,
bearing with one another in love" (Ephesians 4:2).*

MAX LUCADO

Opening Reflection

We are called to accept one another even when we have major disagreements on big issues. But we are also called to accept one another in the little things. When someone rubs you the wrong way, cuts in line, or laughs too loud. Even when someone commits your *worst* pet peeve—whatever that may happen to be—you are called to "be patient, bearing with one another in love" (Ephesians 4:2).

Bearing with one another can be more difficult than accepting one another. It can be easy to make sweeping statements such as, "I am a Republican, but I respect Democrats." It can be far more difficult to continue to love your spouse even when he's left the toilet seat up for the umpteenth time. But letting your pet peeves get to you is a sure path to unhappiness. When pet peeves rule the day, so do annoyance, anger, and unnecessary grudges.

On the other hand, when you commit to being patient and bearing with one another, you strip your pet peeves of their power. Patience allows you to give your loved one a second chance . . . and a third . . . and a fourth. A smile comes to your face more easily. You are free from your pet peeves and free to accept others in the big disagreements and in the small.

And here's a secret about bearing with one another: people have to bear with you too. Yes, *you*. You have quirks. You leave

34

your shoes all over the house. You drive under the speed limit in the left lane. You commit someone else's pet peeve on a daily basis. As you work to bear with the people around you, remember, they are also working to bear with you.

Jesus left a prime example of how to bear with one another. He took things one step further. He didn't simply tolerate others but *loved* them and *encouraged* them to be the best versions of themselves. Pay attention to the words and actions of Jesus in this session and see how the One who accepted you—sin and all—can teach you to do the same to others.

Talk About It

If you or any of your group members are just meeting for the first time, take a few minutes to introduce yourselves and share any insights you have from last week's personal study. Next, to get things started for the group time, discuss one of the following questions:

- What is your biggest pet peeve?

—or—

- Why are pet peeves so annoying?

Hearing the Word

Invite someone to read aloud Matthew 7:3–5. Listen for fresh insights as you hear the verses being read, and then discuss the questions that follow.

[3] Why do you notice the little piece of dust in your friend's eye, but you don't notice the big piece of wood in your own eye? [4] How can you say to your friend, "Let me take that little piece of dust out of your eye"? Look at yourself! You still have that big piece of wood in your own eye. [5] You hypocrite! First, take the wood out of your own eye. Then you will see clearly to take the dust out of your friend's eye (NCV).

What is one key insight that stands out to you from this passage?

In what ways did that represent a new insight?

Do you tend to focus on your faults or the faults of others?

Video Teaching Notes

Play the video segment for session two. As you watch, use the following outline to record any thoughts or concepts that stand out to you.

We all feel there is a certain way people should behave . . . and when people don't act that way, we call it a "pet peeve."

Paul's word for *patience* is a term that combines *long* and *tempered*.[6] In other words, patient people are not quickly overheated.

The next time you find it difficult to live with others, imagine what it is like to live with you.

We have eagle-eye vision when it comes to others but can be blind as moles when examining ourselves. So before you go pointing out the specks in the eyes of others, make sure you aren't sporting a sequoia limb in your own.

You would want any constructive criticism you receive to actually be *constructive*. Bearing with one another is thus best accomplished by mixing in some encouragement about what the person is doing *right*.

Jesus did with Peter what encouragers do. He called him out. He built Peter up. With the skill of a rock mason, he stacked stones of affirmation and inspiration upon his disciple.

Jesus gave his full attention to the desperate woman who came to see him. In spite of the pressing crowds, an errand to heal a sick girl, and questioning disciples, Jesus stopped what he was doing and listened. And then he *affirmed* her.

Ask to hear other people's stories. Resist the urge to interrupt them. Give them the rarest of gifts: your full attention.

Group Discussion

Take a few minutes with your group members to discuss what you just watched and explore these concepts in Scripture.

1. How do you typically react when someone does that one thing that *really* gets on your nerves? How does this affect your mood and overall happiness?

After all the hard work we had put into our home, it was suddenly gone. It was literally under concrete. The situation was unbearable, but once we got settled into our new lives, we quickly realized we had been so worried about the foundation in our house that we hadn't understood the foundation that really needed work was our marriage. It was like God's little joke, saying, "Okay, your priorities are messed up. Let's get you refocused." I remember when the contractor called and said the home was ready. We walked in, and it didn't even look like our house. It was the greatest thing that's ever happened to us, because we were renewed, we were happier than we had been that whole first year we were married. And we got this brand-new house that looked exactly how we envisioned.

— JESSICA & CHASE, FROM THE VIDEO

2. In Ephesians 4:2, Paul instructed us to be "patient" or "long-tempered" with one another. What does it mean to be long-tempered? Would you say this type of patience comes naturally for you? Why or why not?

3. In Matthew 7:3–5, Jesus instructed us to examine ourselves before we examine others. How would examining yourself first help you to bear with others? What are some of *your* quirks that might get on their nerves?

4. Do you think Jesus had to be patient and bear with his disciples? How do you think Jesus—who was God made flesh—was able to be patient with those around him?

5. Read Matthew 16:17. How did Jesus encourage Peter in this verse? How do you think this made Peter feel?

6. Read Mark 5:25-34. How did Jesus encourage the sick woman? Have you ever felt encouraged by someone who listened to you? How did that person encourage you?

7. How did Jessica and Chase ultimately turn their marriage in a healthy direction? Does any part of their story resonate with you? If so, which part and why?

8. Think of someone in your life with whom you need to be more patient. How could you exercise more patience with that person this week?

Closing Activity

To apply today's study, complete the Scripture exercise below:

- *Fill in the blank with the name of someone with whom you have difficulty being patient:* "Be completely humble and gentle; be patient, bearing with _____ in love" (Ephesians 4:2).

- *Fill in the blank with the name of someone you need to encourage this week:* "Let us consider how we may spur _____ on toward love and good deeds" (Hebrews 10:24).

- *Fill in the blanks again with the name of that person:* "Therefore encourage _____ and build _____ up" (1 Thessalonians 5:11). Consider how you could deliver this encouragement to that person this week (for example, by sending a text message, going to coffee, or mailing a handwritten note).

If you feel comfortable, share with your group what this experience was like for you.

Closing Prayer

Close your time by spending time with your heavenly Father. Have three different people in the group read one of the prayers below:

- **Gratitude:** God, we thank you for giving us this time together to be in community with one another and with you. Thank you for showing us patience. Thank you for giving us a fresh chance every day to start anew.

- **Petition:** Lord, help us be more patient this week. Give us your Spirit to calm us and remind us that we need to be shown patience as well. Forgive us when we are short-tempered. Help us to be long-tempered.

- **Worship:** We praise you for being our creator and our redeemer. We worship you for who you are, for what you have done, and for what you will do. In Jesus' name we pray. Amen.

Between-Sessions Personal Study

Session Two

Reflect on the material you've covered this week in *How Happiness Happens* by engaging in any or all of the following between-sessions activities. Each personal study consists of four days of reflection activities to help you implement what you learned in the group time. The time you invest will be well spent, so let God use it to draw you closer to him. At your next meeting, share any key points or insights that stood out to you as you spent this time with the Lord.

True Patience

During your group time, you talked about how happiness happens when you do as Paul instructed the believers in Ephesus: "Be patient, bearing with one another in love" (Ephesians 4:2). As you discussed, the Greek word translated for *patience*, *makrothumia*,[7] means *long-tempered*. It can also mean *long-suffering*, *steadfastness*, *endurance*, and *constancy*. These definitions suggest that patience is more than a one-time reaction—it is a consistent way of being. How can you become more patient? Begin by reading Galatians 5:19–25:

> [19] Now the deeds of the flesh are evident, which are: immorality, impurity, sensuality, [20] idolatry, sorcery, enmities, strife, jealousy, outbursts of anger, disputes, dissensions, factions, [21] envying, drunkenness, carousing, and things like these, of which I forewarn you, just as I have forewarned you, that those who practice such things will not inherit the kingdom of God. [22] But the fruit of the Spirit is love, joy, peace, patience, kindness, goodness, faithfulness, [23] gentleness, self-control; against such things there is no law. [24] Now those who belong to Christ Jesus have crucified the flesh with its passions and desires. [25] If we live by the Spirit, let us also walk by the Spirit (NASB).

1. What are some of the deeds of the flesh? What will happen if you commit deeds of the flesh (see verses 19–21)?

2. What are some of the fruit of the Spirit? What happens when you exhibit that fruit in your life?

3. Think about how an apple tree grows. What are the stages of growth from seed to fruit? Considering this, how do you bear the fruit of patience? How does it grow in you?

4. According to verse 25, how does Paul say that you should live and walk?

5. The book of Psalms opens with these words on the subject of happiness:

> [1] Happy are those who do not follow the advice of the wicked, or take the path that sinners tread, or sit in the seat of scoffers; [2] but their delight is in the law of the Lord, and on his law they meditate day and night. [3] They are like trees planted by streams of water, which yield their fruit in its season, and their leaves do not wither. In all that they do, they prosper (1:1–3 NRSV).

According to this passage, in what does a happy person delight? On what does a happy person meditate?

6. What metaphor does the psalmist use in this passage to describe the happy person whose delight is in the law of the Lord?

7. How can you live and walk by the Spirit? When you delight in the Lord and meditate on his Word, what will happen (see verse 3)?

8. How does this passage help you understand the way you can produce the fruit of the Spirit that Paul wrote about in Galatians 5:22–23?

9. What is an area of your life where you could use more patience?

10. How could a practice of reading Scripture or focusing on God help you to produce this fruit of the Spirit?

Prayer: *In your prayer time today, reflect on Psalm 1:1–3. Offer it as a prayer to God. Ask him to reveal new insights to you. Ask him to transform your heart according to his Word.*

A Change of Perspective

Patience is key to our happiness, but being patient is not always easy. Sometimes, a change of perspective is needed for us to be patient with the people in our lives. When we remember that others have to bear with us, we are quicker to bear with them. Today, spend more time in Matthew 7:1–5 to learn how to change your perspective and be more patient with others.

> [1] Don't judge others, or you will be judged. [2] You will be judged in the same way that you judge others, and the amount you give to others will be given to you.
> [3] Why do you notice the little piece of dust in your friend's eye, but you don't notice the big piece of wood in your own eye? [4] How can you say to your friend, "Let me take that little piece of dust out of your eye"? Look at yourself! You still have that big piece of wood in your own eye. [5] You hypocrite! First, take the wood out of your own eye. Then you will see clearly to take the dust out of your friend's eye (NCV).

1. According to this passage, why shouldn't you judge others?

2. Have you ever felt judged by someone else? How did it make you feel? How did you feel about the person who judged you?

3. Think about the last time you judged someone. For what did you judge that person? Looking back, how could you have examined yourself before judging him or her?

4. If you're being impatient with those around you, it could be because you're impatient with yourself. Think about some of the ways you judge yourself (for example, for not working hard enough, for being a "bad" parent, or for not being a good friend). How do the ways you judge yourself affect the way you judge others?

5. The pendulum can easily swing from judging yourself to judging others to judging yourself again. This is why it is important to be grounded in who *God* says you are—to

know that he created you with innate value. As David writes in Psalm 139:13-14:

[13] Oh yes, you shaped me first inside, then out; you formed me in my mother's womb. [14] I thank you, High God—you're breathtaking! Body and soul, I am marvelously made! I worship in adoration—what a creation! (MSG).

How does David describe the way you were made? What is his response to his own creation by God?

6. When you look at yourself in the mirror, what thoughts do you have about yourself? When you look at other people, what thoughts do you have about them?

7. How would it affect the way you think about yourself if you truly accepted that you were marvelously made? How would it affect the way you interact with others?

Prayer: *As you interact with others (family, friends, coworkers), consider what God says about them—that they are wondrously and marvelously made. Pray that these individuals would feel encouraged, comforted, and guided today by the Holy Spirit. Say a prayer thanking God for the many diverse people in your life.*

Build Up and Call Out

When you focus on encouraging others, you are able to bear with them and appreciate them for their unique value. As Paul wrote in 1 Thessalonians 5:11, "Therefore encourage one another and build each other up." The noun form of the Greek word translated as *encourage* is *paraklesis*, which is a combination of two words: *para*, which means "by the side," and *kaleo*, which means "to call."[8] In other words, biblical encouragement includes coming alongside someone and calling out the good you see in that person.

1. Who in your life has encouraged you in the *paraklesis* kind of way? How did that person encourage you? What did he or she say?

2. How did this encouragement affect the way you thought about yourself?

3. In Matthew 16:13–19, we read how Jesus encouraged Peter with the *paraklesis* kind of encouragement when the disciples were in the region of Caesarea Philippi:

   [13] When Jesus came into the region of Caesarea Philippi, He asked His disciples, saying, "Who do men say that I, the Son of Man, am?"

[14] So they said, "Some say John the Baptist, some Elijah, and others Jeremiah or one of the prophets."
[15] He said to them, "But who do you say that I am?"
[16] Simon Peter answered and said, "You are the Christ, the Son of the living God."
[17] Jesus answered and said to him, "Blessed are you, Simon Bar-Jonah, for flesh and blood has not revealed this to you, but My Father who is in heaven. [18] And I also say to you that you are Peter, and on this rock I will build My church, and the gates of Hades shall not prevail against it. [19] And I will give you the keys of the kingdom of heaven, and whatever you bind on earth will be bound in heaven, and whatever you loose on earth will be loosed in heaven" (NKJV).

How did Jesus encourage Peter in verses 17–18?

4. Verse 19 in *The Message* translation reads, "And that's not all. You will have complete and free access to God's kingdom, keys to open any and every door: no more barriers between heaven and earth, earth and heaven. A yes on earth is yes in heaven. A no on earth is no in heaven." How was this an encouragement to Peter?

5. What would it be like to be encouraged by Christ himself in the same way Peter was in this passage? What would you want to hear from Jesus?

6. Who is someone in your life you could encourage in the same way Jesus encouraged Peter? What are some ways you could encourage that person?

7. In Hebrews 3:12–13, the author also uses the Greek term *paraklesis* to describe the way in which believers should encourage one another:

> [12] See to it, brothers and sisters, that none of you has a sinful, unbelieving heart that turns away from the living God. [13] But encourage one another daily, as long as it is called "Today," so that none of you may be hardened by sin's deceitfulness.

What does the author of Hebrews urge his readers to do (see verse 12)? How does encouragement play a part?

8. Notice the word *today* in verse 13. What does this tell you about the urgency of this command? Why is encouraging one another *now* so important?

Prayer: *During this week's group time, you wrote down the name of someone in your life who needs encouragement right now. Think about ways in which you could encourage that person this week— and then put those ideas into action. Pray today that God would continue to build up that person and give him or her confidence in whatever he or she is facing.*

Further Reflection

Reflect on what you studied this week: having patience with others, reserving judgment of others and yourself, and encouraging others. Journal your thoughts or write them as a prayer to God, whether you need to ask him questions about what you learned, thank him for what you learned, or ask him what to do next now that you have a better understanding of these topics in Scripture. Also write down any observations or questions that you want to bring to your next group time.

For Next Week: In preparation for next week, read chapters 4 and 7 in *How Happiness Happens*.

Session Three

Serve One Another

*As believers in Christ, we have the freedom to "do good"
unto others—and the research is clear that as we do, it does a
lot of good to ourselves. It is actually in our best interests to
look out for the interests of others. Happiness happens not
when we seek to bring joy to ourselves but as we embody this
simple principle from Paul: "Brethren . . . do not use liberty as
an opportunity for the flesh, but through love serve one
another" (Galatians 5:13 NKJV).*

MAX LUCADO

Opening Reflection

Jesus' teachings were full of paradoxes—ideas that were countercultural to the way things had always been done:

> "But I tell you, do not resist an evil person. If anyone slaps you on the right cheek, turn to them the other cheek also" (Matthew 5:39).

> "If anyone wants to sue you and takes your shirt, hand over your coat as well" (5:40).

> "The last will be first, and the first will be last" (20:16).

In today's study, you will explore a similar paradox given by Paul in his letter to the Philippians: "With humility of mind regard one another as more important than yourselves" (2:3 NASB). In the same vein, Paul also instructs his readers not to use their newfound liberty in Christ in a selfish way, "but through love serve one another" (Galatians 5:13 NKJV).

In a world where the conversation is all about self-care, it is easy to overlook the value of serving others and viewing them as more important than ourselves. The message from our culture is if you're feeling unhappy, you should focus more on your own happiness. Take a vacation, get a massage, eat an ice cream cone.

While taking care of ourselves and enjoying simple pleasures isn't wrong, we can take self-care to the extreme of self-focus. And too much self-focus does not bring happiness but rather self-destruction. When we examine our lives under a microscope, we are sure to see everything that is wrong with our situation. On the other hand, when we focus on serving others, we can zoom out of our own lives and see others' lives more clearly. The question changes from *"What do I need?"* to *"What do they need?"*

As we practice the act of serving others, we realize making someone else smile brings a smile to our own faces. As the prophet Isaiah wrote, "If you spend yourselves in behalf of the hungry and satisfy the needs of the oppressed, then your light will rise in the darkness, and your night will become like the noonday" (58:10). Doing good truly does the doer good.

Seeking joy by serving others is a little counterintuitive, a little upside down, a little paradoxical. Yet this is often the way of Christ—who, by the way, once said, "The Son of Man did not come to be served, but to serve, and to give his life as a ransom for many" (Mark 10:45).

Talk About It

Begin your group time by inviting anyone to share his or her insights from last week's personal study. Next, to get things started, discuss one of the following questions:

- What are some of the most memorable things that others have done as acts of service for you?

—or—

- What are some of the most memorable ways that you have served others?

Hearing the Word

Invite someone to read aloud Matthew 20:26–28. Listen for fresh insights as you hear the verses being read, and then discuss the questions that follow.

> [26] Whoever wants to become great among you must be your servant, [27] and whoever wants to be first must be your slave— [28] just as the Son of Man did not come to be served, but to serve, and to give his life as a ransom for many.

What is one key insight that stands out to you from this passage?

In what ways did that represent a new insight?

Who is someone you consider to be great? Who is someone you consider to be a servant?

Video Teaching Notes

Play the video segment for session three. As you watch, use the following outline to record any thoughts or concepts that stand out to you.

It is in your best interest to look out for the interests of others! The way to make yourself smile is to first make someone else smile.

The Bible has its share of saints spurred by a gut-level conviction that God had called them to a specific task. As a result, their work wasn't affected by moods, cloudy days, or rocky trails.

Anyone who appreciates Paul's epistles owes a debt of gratitude to Peter. And anyone who has benefited from the faith of Peter owes a debt to the servant spirit of Andrew.

To describe Epaphroditus, Paul used words like *brother, co-worker, fellow soldier,* and *messenger.* These are compliments earned over years and tears.

Let all unassuming people of the world be reminded: God can *use* you. And let all proud people be cautioned: God will *correct* you.

We are valuable to God, but not indispensable. We do nothing apart from the hand of God. It's a principle Jesus had to teach to two of his own disciples: James and John.

After the resurrection, we read how Jesus, the unrivaled Commander of the Universe, invited his friends to sit down and have a bite to eat. What's more, he does the same for us today.

What would happen if everyone truly decided to take on the role of a servant by turning the focus off themselves and putting it on others?

Group Discussion

Take a few minutes with your group members to discuss what you just watched and explore these concepts in Scripture.

1. When you are feeling low, sad, or depressed, what do you typically do to try to make yourself feel better? Does it work? Why or why not?

Getting closer to the wedding, it felt like a cloud was hanging over my fiancé and me. Slowly things were unraveling. And with each setback, I tried to fix it myself. But at one point, God revealed to me, "You know what? This is not the right person." So I had to cancel the flowers, the cake . . . everything. And it just came to me that, "Well, I can't use these things, but somebody else can. So why waste all of it?" It impacted me a lot to give these things from my wedding away—to serve my community in any way that I can. It brought me so much joy, even in a day that unraveled before my eyes, that I was able to provide help in different ways. It helped me restore my happiness. Slowly, I've regained my joy and my sense of peace.

JOANNA, FROM THE VIDEO

2. When you think about the heroes in the Bible, who comes to mind? In what ways did those individuals exhibit humility and service to others?

3. What characteristics do people in our culture tend to value today? Why do you think our society places such an emphasis on possessing those characteristics?

4. Before today's video segment, what did you know about Andrew and Epaphroditus in the New Testament? By today's standards and culture, how would people treat or view someone like Andrew or Epaphroditus?

5. Read Galatians 5:13. *Freedom* is typically considered the opposite of *serving*, but here Paul says that freedom in Christ frees us to serve. How can the freedom we have in Christ lead us to serve others? In what ways have you experienced this in your life?

6. Read Philippians 2:3. How did Jesus follow this principle in the Gospels?

7. Read Matthew 6:1. Why is it important to examine our *motives* when we serve others? What is the problem with serving in order to bring attention to ourselves?

8. Joanna was able to turn something difficult into an opportunity to serve. What is a practical way you could serve others the next time you are feeling down?

Closing Activity

To apply today's study, complete the Scripture exercise below:

- *Fill in the blank with the name of someone who could benefit from your gifts and talents:* "Use whatever gift you have received to serve _____, as faithful stewards of God's grace in its various forms" (1 Peter 4:10).

- *Fill in the blank with the name of someone who needs encouragement and support today:* "Dear children, let us not love _____ with words or speech but with actions and in truth" (1 John 3:18).

- *Fill in the blank with the name of a person you know who is in need today:* "Look after _____ in their distress" (James 1:27).

Take this to the next level by brainstorming some ways your group could actively serve your community. Some ideas include serving at a local food bank, serving in the nursery or children's department in your church, or even helping neighbors clean up their lawns. Coordinate an evening or weekend with your group when the members could participate in this service project.

Closing Prayer

Close your time by spending time with your heavenly Father. Have someone lead your group in prayer, asking God to provide you with greater opportunities to serve others. Or have someone in the group read the following prayer aloud:

> *God, we confess that we often regard ourselves as more important than others. We do not serve when we should because we are focused on our own needs. Help us see the needs of others. Help us to regard others as more important than ourselves. Give us opportunities throughout the week to notice the needs of others and work to meet them. Thank you for sending us your Son, Jesus, as the ultimate example of a servant. May we see others as he saw them, may we act toward others as he acted toward them, and may we love them as he loved them. In Jesus' name we pray. Amen.*

Between-Sessions Personal Study

Session Three

Reflect on the material you've covered this week in *How Happiness Happens* by engaging in any or all of the following between-sessions activities. Each personal study consists of four days of reflection activities to help you implement what you learned in the group time. The time you invest will be well spent, so let God use it to draw you closer to him. At your next meeting, share any key points or insights that stood out to you as you spent this time with the Lord.

Who Was Jesus?

During your group time you talked about how happiness happens when we serve others. We often forget that Jesus came to serve us—even laying down his life for us—but this is an important part of who Christ was and what this means for us today. Before you begin today's study, think about how you would describe Jesus. What words or adjectives come to mind? Next, spend some time looking at how Jesus is described as a servant in the Bible by reading the following verses. As you read, underline any words or phrases that stand out to you:

> The Son of Man did not come to be served, but to serve (Matthew 20:28).

> Follow God's example, therefore, as dearly loved children and walk in the way of love, just as Christ loved us and gave himself up for us as a fragrant offering and sacrifice to God (Ephesians 5:1–2).

> Jesus Christ . . . gave himself for us to redeem us from all lawlessness and to purify for himself a people for his own possession who are zealous for good works (Titus 2:13–14 ESV).

1. What did Christ come to earth to do (see Matthew 20:28)? What did he *not* come to earth to do?

2. How did Jesus show his love for us (see Ephesians 5:1–2)?

3. Why did Jesus give himself up for us (see Titus 2:13–14)?

4. Read these other descriptions of Jesus that are found in the Bible:

> For unto us a Child is born, unto us a Son is given; and the government will be upon His shoulder. And His name will be called Wonderful, Counselor, Mighty God, Everlasting Father, Prince of Peace (Isaiah 9:6 NKJV).

> The angel said to them ... "To you is born this day in the city of David a Savior, who is the Messiah, the Lord" (Luke 2:10–11 NRSV).

> The Word became flesh and dwelt among us, and we beheld His glory, the glory as of the only begotten of the Father, full of grace and truth (John 1:14 NKJV).

How is Jesus described in the prophecy of Isaiah (see Isaiah 9:6)?

5. How does the angel describe Jesus (see Luke 2:10–11)?

6. How does John describe Jesus in his Gospel (see John 1:15)?

7. Jesus was a true example of servant leadership—someone who led others by first serving them. In Luke 5:17–26, we read about his encounter with a paralytic man:

[17] Now it happened on a certain day, as He was teaching, that there were Pharisees and teachers of the law sitting by, who had come out of every town of Galilee, Judea, and Jerusalem. And the power of the Lord was present to heal them. [18] Then behold, men brought on a bed a man who was paralyzed, whom they sought to bring in and lay before Him. [19] And when they could not find how they might bring him in, because of the crowd, they went up on the housetop and let him down with his bed through the tiling into the midst before Jesus.

[20] When He saw their faith, He said to him, "Man, your sins are forgiven you."

[21] And the scribes and the Pharisees began to reason, saying, "Who is this who speaks blasphemies? Who can forgive sins but God alone?"

[22] But when Jesus perceived their thoughts, He answered and said to them, "Why are you reasoning in your hearts? [23] Which is easier, to say, 'Your sins are forgiven you,' or to say, 'Rise up and walk'? [24] But that you may know that the Son of Man has power on earth to forgive sins"—He said to the man who was paralyzed, "I say to you, arise, take up your bed, and go to your house."

[25] Immediately he rose up before them, took up what he had been lying on, and departed to his own house, glorifying God. [26] And they were all amazed,

and they glorified God and were filled with fear, saying, "We have seen strange things today!" (NKJV).

How did Jesus serve others in this story?

8. How did Jesus prove his power and authority?

9. Does Jesus' example of servant-leadership challenge any previous notions you've had about what it takes to be a leader? If so, what notions?

10. Considering the passages you've just read, how would you *now* describe Jesus?

Prayer: *End your time reading your answer to the last question as a prayer of worship to Jesus. Tell him who he is. Tell him you are grateful for who he was in Scripture. Tell him that you are grateful that he is still the same today. Ask him to make you more like him.*

Whom Did Jesus Serve?

The Gospels are filled with stories of how Jesus served and ministered to the people wherever he went. Begin by reading a few of these stories found in the following passages:

[12] It happened when He was in a certain city, that behold, a man who was full of leprosy saw Jesus; and he fell on his face and implored Him, saying, "Lord, if You are willing, You can make me clean." [13] Then He put out His hand and touched him, saying, "I am willing; be cleansed." Immediately the leprosy left him (Luke 5:12–13 NKJV).

[5] When Jesus reached the spot, he looked up and said to him, "Zacchaeus, come down immediately. I must stay at your house today." [6] So he came down at once and welcomed him gladly. [7] All the people saw this and began to mutter, "He has gone to be the guest of a sinner." [8] But Zacchaeus stood up and said to the Lord, "Look, Lord! Here and now I give half of my possessions to the poor, and if I have cheated anybody out of anything, I will pay back four times the amount." [9] Jesus said to him, "Today salvation has come to this house, because this man, too, is a son of Abraham. [10] For the Son of Man came to seek and to save the lost" (Luke 19:5–10).

[9] As soon as they had come to land, they saw a fire of coals there, and fish laid on it, and bread. [10] Jesus said to them, "Bring some of the fish which you have just

caught." [11] Simon Peter went up and dragged the net to land, full of large fish, one hundred and fifty-three; and although there were so many, the net was not broken. [12] Jesus said to them, "Come and eat breakfast." Yet none of the disciples dared ask Him, "Who are You?"—knowing that it was the Lord. [13] Jesus then came and took the bread and gave it to them, and likewise the fish (John 21:9–13 NKJV).

1. What request did the man who had leprosy make in Luke 5:12-13? How did Jesus respond to the man's request?

2. How did Jesus react when he saw Zacchaeus in Luke 19:5-10? How did Jesus respond to the people's claim that he had gone to be the guest of a sinner?

3. Who did Jesus serve in John 21:12-13? Why was even this simple act significant (see Mark 14:44–50)?

4. What do these verses tell you about the kinds of people Jesus was willing to serve?

5. What do these verses tell you about the way Jesus viewed all people?

6. Are there some people in your life who are easier for you to serve than others? If so, who is easy for you to serve? Who is difficult for you to serve? Why?

7. In these passages, we see Jesus serving a man with leprosy (a group shunned by society), interacting with sinners (a group also shunned by society), and serving breakfast to his disciples (who had abandoned him in his time of need). While there is no limit to whom Jesus will serve, these stories reveal that Jesus does tend to give special attention to those on the margins of society (see also Mark 5:25–34 and John 4:3–26). Why do you think Jesus went out of his way to serve these types of people?

8. What people in your community live on the "margins"?

9. Are you actively serving these people in any way? Why or why not?

10. If you're not already serving people on the margins in your community, think of some groups or organizations you know of who are serving these communities. Is there an opportunity for you to work with any of these groups or organizations? If so, what will you commit to doing this week or this month to serve?

Prayer: *Thank God for sending Jesus to serve you. Thank Jesus for giving his life as a ransom for many—including you. Ask God for an opportunity to serve in your community. Ask him to put a person, or a group of people, on your heart and to open doors for you to serve. Ask him to give you everything you need to serve these people—time, energy, love, and compassion.*

How Did Jesus Serve?

As we have seen, Jesus healed the sick, broke bread with the disciples, and reached out to those who were typically neglected by society. Yet Jesus' ultimate act of service happened on the cross. As Paul wrote, "[God] made Him who knew no sin to be sin for us, that we might become the righteousness of God in Him" (2 Corinthians 5:21 NKJV). Read each of the following passages about this ultimate act of service, and then answer the questions that follow.

Praying in the Garden

> ³⁶ Then Jesus came with them to a place called Geth-
> semane, and said to the disciples, "Sit here while I go
> and pray over there." ³⁷ And He took with Him Peter
> and the two sons of Zebedee, and He began to be sor-
> rowful and deeply distressed. ³⁸ Then He said to them,
> "My soul is exceedingly sorrowful, even to death. Stay
> here and watch with Me."
>
> ³⁹ He went a little farther and fell on His face, and
> prayed, saying, "O My Father, if it is possible, let this
> cup pass from Me; nevertheless, not as I will, but as
> You will" (Matthew 26:36–39 NKJV).

1. How was Jesus feeling about the events that were to come
   (see verse 38)?

2. What was Jesus' attitude as he approached this time (see
   verse 39)?

Betrayed by a Friend

> ⁴⁷ Judas, one of the Twelve, arrived. With him was a
> large crowd armed with swords and clubs, sent from

the chief priests and the elders of the people. [48] Now the betrayer had arranged a signal with them: "The one I kiss is the man; arrest him." [49] Going at once to Jesus, Judas said, "Greetings, Rabbi!" and kissed him.

[50] Jesus replied, "Do what you came for, friend." Then the men stepped forward, seized Jesus and arrested him (Matthew 26:47–50).

3. Judas, as one of Jesus' disciples, had been ministering with Christ for the last three years. How do you think it felt for Jesus to be betrayed by him?

4. Jesus served Judas even though he knew Judas would eventually betray him. Have you ever been betrayed by a friend? How would it feel for you to serve that friend?

Wrongfully Convicted

[22] "What shall I do, then, with Jesus who is called the Messiah?" Pilate asked.

They all answered, "Crucify him!"

[23] "Why? What crime has he committed?" asked Pilate.

But they shouted all the louder, "Crucify him!"

²⁴ When Pilate saw that he was getting nowhere, but that instead an uproar was starting, he took water and washed his hands in front of the crowd. "I am innocent of this man's blood," he said. "It is your responsibility!"

²⁵ All the people answered, "His blood is on us and on our children!"

²⁶ Then he released Barabbas to them. But he had Jesus flogged, and handed him over to be crucified (Matthew 27:22–26).

5. Have you ever been wrongfully accused of something? If so, how did you respond?

6. Why do you think Jesus accepted this punishment he didn't deserve? What does this tell you about his willingness to serve?

Forsaken on the Cross

⁴⁵ From noon until three in the afternoon darkness came over all the land. ⁴⁶ About three in the afternoon Jesus cried out in a loud voice, "Eli, Eli, lema sabachthani?" (which means "My God, my God, why have you forsaken me?").

⁴⁷ When some of those standing there heard this, they said, "He's calling Elijah."

⁴⁸ Immediately one of them ran and got a sponge. He filled it with wine vinegar, put it on a staff, and offered it to Jesus to drink. ⁴⁹ The rest said, "Now leave him alone. Let's see if Elijah comes to save him."

⁵⁰ And when Jesus had cried out again in a loud voice, he gave up his spirit (Matthew 27:45–50).

7. What were Jesus' feelings as he hung on the cross (see verse 46)?

8. Why did Jesus submit to God's plan even though he knew it meant he would be forsaken?

9. What does the story of Jesus' crucifixion tell us about the type of servant he was?

10. The cross was Jesus' greatest expression of love for us. He died so that we might have eternal life (see John 3:16). How could the knowledge of this love encourage you to better serve others?

Prayer: *Thank Jesus for his sacrifice, love, and devotion to you, even though you are a sinner. Ask God for a deeper understanding of what Jesus' sacrifice means for your life. Ask God that you would be transformed by the deep and eternal love of Christ and that his love would reach others through you.*

Further Reflection

Reflect on what you studied this week: Jesus as a servant-leader, the kinds of people Jesus served, and the ways in which Jesus served—culminating in his ultimate act of service on the cross. Journal your thoughts or write them as a prayer to God, whether you need to ask him questions about what you learned, thank him for what you learned, or ask him what to do next now that you have a better understanding of these topics in Scripture. Also write down any observations or questions that you want to bring to your next group time.

For Next Week: In preparation for next week, read chapter 10 in *How Happiness Happens*.

Session Four

Forgive One Another

*The story of the prodigal son reveals that nothing
stirs the passion of God quite like seeing his kids in the pigsty.
Nothing moves his hand such as seeing his desperate sons
and daughters drooling for corncobs but longing to be home.
And when they do come home, they receive the same
response as the prodigal received: forgiveness and
acceptance. Regardless of what we've done, when God sees
us make a turn toward home, he runs to receive us. It is in this
context that Paul urges each of us to follow suit: "Be kind to
one another, tenderhearted, forgiving one another, even as
God in Christ forgave you" (Ephesians 4:32 NKJV).*

MAX LUCADO

Opening Reflection

Who is on your "list"? You know the list. Many of us have one, even if we're not conscious of it. The List of People Who Have Hurt Us. Who is on yours? Perhaps your list includes old friends, siblings, or parents. Maybe you no longer speak to some of the people on your list, or you avoid them, or you're holding a grudge against them.

It is natural to feel angry with someone who hurt you. What is not so natural is to forgive. Yet forgiveness is one of the greatest callings of the Christian life. Paul said as much to the believers in the church in Ephesus: "Be kind to one another, tenderhearted, forgiving one another, even as God in Christ forgave you" (Ephesians 4:32 NKJV).

We often withhold forgiveness for fear of letting the wrongdoer off the hook. We are a society of right and wrong, checks and balances, justice and punishment. If we forgive someone who said that thing to us or did that thing to us, it feels unfair. We reason to ourselves that people should have to pay for what they've done to us.

But the gospel tells a different story. When Jesus died on the cross, he created a new way. His ultimate act of forgiveness for our sins allows us to forgive others—not because they deserve it, but because we have been forgiven. This is why

Paul says to forgive "as God in Christ forgave you." In light of the cross, forgiveness is less an act that lets our offender off the hook and more a response to the forgiveness that we have received.

When we fully grasp the depth and breadth of God's grace and mercy toward us, forgiveness—while still difficult—at least becomes possible. And so does happiness. After all, how happy do we really feel when we are angry with another person? How happy do we feel when we are harboring a years-old grudge? Withholding forgiveness takes a toll on our happiness. Forgiveness rids us of the grudge, the angst, the tension, and frees us to feel happy again.

As you work through this session, think about who you need to forgive in your life. Also think about how you've been forgiven. And thank God for the grace he has given you to give to others.

Talk About It

Begin your group time by inviting anyone to share his or her insights from last week's personal study. Next, to get things started, discuss one of the following questions:

- What do think about the phrase "forgive and forget"? Are they words to live by or a pipe dream? Why?

—*or*—

- When was the last time you forgave someone? Why did you need to forgive this person?

Hearing the Word

Invite someone to read aloud John 13:12–17. Listen for fresh insights as you hear the verses being read, and then discuss the questions that follow.

> [12] So when He had washed their feet, taken His garments, and sat down again, He said to them, "Do you know what I have done to you? [13] You call Me Teacher and Lord, and you say well, for so I am. [14] If I then, your Lord and Teacher, have washed your feet, you also ought to wash one another's feet. [15] For I have given you an example, that you should do as I have done to you. [16] Most assuredly, I say to you, a servant is not greater than his master; nor is he who is sent greater than he who sent him. [17] If you know these things, blessed are you if you do them (NKJV).

What is one key insight that stands out to you from this passage?

In what ways did that represent a new insight?

What knowledge does Jesus say will make us blessed? Why would we be blessed for knowing these things?

Video Teaching Notes

Play the video segment for session four. As you watch, use the following outline to record any thoughts or concepts that stand out to you.

Forgiveness is an important principle to grasp, because we have all suffered harm at the hands of another person. The hurt is deep. And it is real.

We need to be realistic about forgiveness. It does not pardon the offense, excuse the misdeed, or condone it. It is simply deciding not to allow the hurt to harden us, numb us, or take our joy.

Jesus knew he was sent from heaven and destined for heaven. He was certain about his identity and destiny, which allowed him to serve his disciples and wash their feet.

How Happiness Happens Study Guide

Jesus repeated the foot-washing on every set of feet. He didn't exclude a single follower—not even the feet of Judas, who would shortly betray him.

Jesus forgave his betrayers *before* they betrayed him. And when we think about it, he has done the same for us.

The story of the prodigal son reveals that regardless of what we've done, when God sees us make a turn toward home, he runs to receive us.

Paul urges you to extend grace not because your offender deserves it but because you've been doused with it. So start the process of forgiveness with a few small steps:

Decide what you need to forgive

84

Ask why it hurts

Take the pain to Jesus

Either tell your offender or pray for your offender

Conduct a funeral

Jesus wants you to take up the towel. Fill up the basin. And wash one another's feet.

Group Discussion

Take a few minutes with your group members to discuss what you just watched and explore these concepts in Scripture.

1. In your own words, what is *forgiveness*? How do you know if you have forgiven someone? How do you know if you haven't forgiven someone yet?

2. Read Ephesians 4:32. What verb tense did Paul use when he instructed us to forgive one another? Why is this significant?

3. Read Matthew 18:21–22. Considering the verb tense in Ephesians 4:32 and Jesus' instruction in this passage, how and when are we to forgive others?

4. Have you ever been forgiven by another person when you didn't deserve forgiveness? If you feel comfortable, share that experience with the group.

After years of issue after issue with our children, whether we spoke it or not, we seemed to feel like we had gotten the bad end of the deal. This wasn't fair, we hadn't signed up for this, and who could we blame? After more years of jail, courtrooms, and judges—which was a new experience for us— we basically wanted to say, "We're done." Something's got to turn. I would tie our experience in with forgiveness and say the beauty for us has been to see that sticking with it day to day— offering our children the same umbrella of forgiveness that God has offered to us—has helped us in living with them and loving them. We live under a covering of forgiveness. Forgiveness just falls into that category of love. It's what Christ did for us, and so it's how we choose to love our kids.

JEFF & CAROL, FROM THE VIDEO

---

5. How did Jesus show forgiveness when he washed the disciples' feet? How did the father in the parable of the prodigal son show forgiveness?

6. Grace is a critical component of the Christian gospel, but it can be a hard concept to grasp. How would you personally define *grace*?

7. Do you feel like you've experienced grace from God? Why or why not?

8. How did Jeff and Carol show grace to their two children? How does this parallel the grace that we have received from God?

Closing Activity

To apply today's study, complete the Scripture exercise below:

- *Fill in the blank with the name of someone whom you need to forgive:* "Bear with each other and forgive _____. . . . Forgive as the Lord forgave you" (Colossians 3:13).

- *Fill in the blank with anything you are currently holding against someone:* "And when you stand praying, if you hold _____ _____ against anyone, forgive them, so that your Father in heaven may forgive you your sins" (Mark 11:25).

- *Fill in the blank with the name of a person whom you've repeatedly had to forgive:* "Even if _____ _____ sin[s] against you seven times in a day and seven times come[s] back to you saying 'I repent,' you must forgive them" (Luke 17:4).

If you feel comfortable, share with your group what this experience was like for you.

Closing Prayer

Close your time by spending time with your heavenly Father. As a group, pray through the following contemplative prayer:

God, we thank you for giving us the opportunity to study your Word. Thank you for the grace and forgiveness you have showed us through Jesus.

We confess that we have not always been quick to forgive and that we hold on to anger and grudges. Forgive us for not forgiving others.

Jesus, we bring to you the pain that others have caused us. We ask you to heal us and show us the path to forgiveness. [Spend several moments in silence.]

Now we lift up the name of our offenders in prayer. Bring them peace. Bring them joy. Give them what they are lacking in their lives. [Spend several moments in silence.]

We recognize that we can only forgive others when we know that we are indeed forgiven. Help us understand the forgiveness and grace you have shown to us. Allow us to feel joy in that forgiveness as we go about our week.

In Jesus' name we pray. Amen.

Between-Sessions Personal Study

Session Four

Reflect on the material you've covered this week in *How Happiness Happens* by engaging in any or all of the following between-sessions activities. Each personal study consists of four days of reflection activities to help you implement what you learned in the group time. The time you invest will be well spent, so let God use it to draw you closer to him. At your next meeting, share any key points or insights that stood out to you as you spent this time with the Lord.

The Forgiveness of Christ

Forgiveness does not start with us. We cannot force ourselves to forgive. When we forgive because we feel we're supposed to do so, or because we think it's the right thing to do, or because we've been told to "forgive and forget," it rarely sticks. We typically hold on to the grudge—we just try to hide it or sweep it under the rug so no one will notice. For this reason, forgiveness must come from a force greater than ourselves.

For the follower of Christ, forgiveness must begin with the grace that God has extended to us through Jesus.

1. How do you understand God's forgiveness through Jesus? (If you're not sure how to answer this question, write down what you're unsure about.)

2. Would you say you have accepted God's forgiveness? Why or why not?

3. In John 13:3–9, we read that on the night that Jesus was betrayed, he met with his disciples in an upper room to celebrate Passover. During that time together, Jesus performed an act of service that startled the disciples—especially Peter:

> [3] Jesus, knowing that the Father had given all things into His hands, and that He had come from God and was going to God, [4] rose from supper and laid aside His garments, took a towel and girded Himself. [5] After that, He poured water into a basin and began to wash the disciples' feet, and to wipe them with the towel with which He was girded. [6] Then He came to Simon Peter. And Peter said to Him, "Lord, are You washing my feet?"

⁷Jesus answered and said to him, "What I am doing you do not understand now, but you will know after this."

⁸Peter said to Him, "You shall never wash my feet!"

Jesus answered him, "If I do not wash you, you have no part with Me."

⁹Simon Peter said to Him, "Lord, not my feet only, but also my hands and my head!" (NKJV).

What are your initial thoughts about this scene? Do you find it odd, touching, confusing, powerful? Explain your answer.

4. What are some of the specific actions that Jesus performed in this passage (see verses 3–5)? What do you think the water and washing symbolize in this passage?

5. What does this metaphor of washing and cleansing tell you about how Jesus has forgiven you?

6. As one scholar notes, "Loosing sandals and personally washing someone else's feet was considered servile, most commonly the work of a servant."[9] What does this tell you about the lengths to which Jesus was willing to go to show forgiveness to the disciples?

7. How did Peter respond to Jesus when he said, "If I do not wash you, you have no part with Me" (verse 8 NKJV)?

8. Imagine that you are in the story. How would you respond to Jesus?

9. After this week's study, do you feel like you better understand what Jesus was doing in this passage and what this means for you today? Explain.

Prayer: *Ask God to reveal what his forgiveness through Christ really means. Thank God for fully forgiving you of your sins. If needed, ask God to help you believe you are fully forgiven.*

The Forgiveness of Self

As previously noted, in order to accept *others*, you first have to accept *yourself*. Forgiveness works in a similar way. If you haven't forgiven yourself for past mistakes, you will find it difficult to extend forgiveness to others. You won't believe you deserve forgiveness—and thus you won't believe that others deserve to be forgiven. However, when you've received the forgiveness of Christ, forgiving yourself comes much more easily and readily.

1. What is something from your past that you still feel guilty about today? How does this guilt affect the way you see yourself?

2. How do you think God feels about this sin, mistake, or incident from your past?

3. In Luke 15:11–24, Jesus told the following story about a prodigal son:

   [11] Jesus continued: "There was a man who had two sons. [12] The younger one said to his father, 'Father, give me my share of the estate.' So he divided his property between them.

[13] "Not long after that, the younger son got together all he had, set off for a distant country and there squandered his wealth in wild living. [14] After he had spent everything, there was a severe famine in that whole country, and he began to be in need. [15] So he went and hired himself out to a citizen of that country, who sent him to his fields to feed pigs. [16] He longed to fill his stomach with the pods that the pigs were eating, but no one gave him anything.

[17] "When he came to his senses, he said, 'How many of my father's hired servants have food to spare, and here I am starving to death! [18] I will set out and go back to my father and say to him: Father, I have sinned against heaven and against you. [19] I am no longer worthy to be called your son; make me like one of your hired servants.' [20] So he got up and went to his father.

"But while he was still a long way off, his father saw him and was filled with compassion for him; he ran to his son, threw his arms around him and kissed him.

[21] "The son said to him, 'Father, I have sinned against heaven and against you. I am no longer worthy to be called your son.'

[22] "But the father said to his servants, 'Quick! Bring the best robe and put it on him. Put a ring on his finger and sandals on his feet. [23] Bring the fattened calf and kill it. Let's have a feast and celebrate. [24] For this son of mine was dead and is alive again; he was lost and is found.' "

How did the son sin against his father (see verses 12–13)?

4. What prompted the prodigal son to return to his father (see verses 14–17)?

5. What did the son plan to say to his father (see 19)? How does this reveal how the son was feeling about himself?

6. Which part of the son's story do you identify with the most—his sin, his motivation for returning home, or the way he viewed himself after he realized that he had messed up? Explain.

7. What three things does the father do upon his son's return (see verse 20)? How does the father describe his son (see verse 24)?

8. Jesus told this story as a parable—a fictional story that reveals an important truth. What truth does this parable reveal?

9. Do you believe this truth applies to you and your past sin? Why or why not?

10. What would it look like for you to forgive yourself in the way the father forgave the son—completely and whole-heartedly? What, if anything, is holding you back from forgiving yourself in this way?

Prayer: *Pray these words as you end your time in the Word: God, thank you for your full forgiveness of my sin. Forgiveness is something I understand in my head, but I don't always believe it in my heart. Help me forgive myself for the sins I've committed in the past. Help me let go and move on. Help me see my sin as dead and no longer a part of the life I live now. Help me to forgive myself so I can forgive others.*

The Forgiveness of Others

As we have seen, forgiveness does not start with us—and it also cannot stop with us. Just as Jesus has forgiven us, we are to go and forgive the people in our lives. When we can do this, we are free to experience joy without anger or a grudge against someone holding us back. Today, begin by reading the first part of the parable of the unforgiving servant told in Matthew 18:21-27:

> [21] Then Peter came to Him and said, "Lord, how often shall my brother sin against me, and I forgive him? Up to seven times?"
>
> [22] Jesus said to him, "I do not say to you, up to seven times, but up to seventy times seven. [23] Therefore the kingdom of heaven is like a certain king who wanted to settle accounts with his servants. [24] And when he had begun to settle accounts, one was brought to him who owed him ten thousand talents. [25] But as he was not able to pay, his master commanded that he be sold, with his wife and children and all that he had, and that payment be made. [26] The servant therefore fell down before him, saying, 'Master, have patience with me, and I will pay you all.' [27] Then the master of that servant was moved with compassion, released him, and forgave him the debt" (NKJV).

1. What is your initial reaction to Jesus' response to Peter's question about how many times he was to forgive (see

verse 22)? Does this instruction seem extreme, fair, impossible? Explain your response.

2. The servant in the parable owed the king 10,000 talents, which was much more than $10,000. One silver talent represented the equivalent of 600 days' wages, so 10,000 talents would be equivalent to sixty million days' wages—more than the king's annual income and more than all of the money in circulation in Egypt at the time.[10] Why do you think Jesus used such a large number to represent the servant's debt?

3. What does the king do for the servant (see verse 27)?

4. What is the king's motivation in taking this particular action?

5. Knowing how much 10,000 talents was worth, what are your thoughts about the king forgiving the servant this vast amount of money?

6. Read the rest of Jesus' parable in Matthew 18:28–35:

> [28] "But that servant went out and found one of his fellow servants who owed him a hundred denarii; and he laid hands on him and took him by the throat, saying, 'Pay me what you owe!' [29] So his fellow servant fell down at his feet and begged him, saying, 'Have patience with me, and I will pay you all.' [30] And he would not, but went and threw him into prison till he should pay the debt. [31] So when his fellow servants saw what had been done, they were very grieved, and came and told their master all that had been done. [32] Then his master, after he had called him, said to him, 'You wicked servant! I forgave you all that debt because you begged me. [33] Should you not also have had compassion on your fellow servant, just as I had pity on you?' [34] And his master was angry, and delivered him to the torturers until he should pay all that was due to him.
>
> [35] "So My heavenly Father also will do to you if each of you, from his heart, does not forgive his brother his trespasses" (NKJV).

How does the servant's response to his fellow servant differ from the king's response (see verse 30)?

7. One hundred denarii was equivalent to 100 days' wages—far less than what the servant owed the king.[11] Why do you think the servant still chose to throw his fellow servant in prison for owing him this amount?

8. How did the king respond when he learned what his servant—whom he had forgiven such a great debt—had done (see verses 32–34)?

9. What truth do you think Jesus was uncovering by telling this parable?

10. During your group session, you spent some time thinking about someone you need to forgive. How are you feeling about forgiving this person in light of this story?

Prayer: *Review the forgiveness exercise discussed in this week's teaching. On an index card, write down the name of someone you need to forgive, and then follow these steps:*

- *Write down what you specifically need to forgive this person for.*
- *Write down why this offense hurt you.*
- *Take the pain to Jesus in prayer.*
- *Consider whether you need to talk to the other person about the offense.*
- *Pray for your offender.*
- *Conduct a funeral for the grievance.*
- *When you are ready, conduct a funeral by burying the index card in your backyard, throwing it in a fire, or simply throwing it away in the trash.*

If you find that you do not have anyone to forgive, just thank God for forgiving you even though your sin is great. Thank him for his compassion and mercy and love. Contemplate how great his mercy and compassion are to forgive all of us our many debts—and ask him to give you the ability to forgive others in the way that you have been forgiven.

Further Reflection

Reflect on what you studied this week: the forgiveness of Christ, forgiving yourself, and forgiving others. Journal your thoughts or write them as a prayer to God, whether you need to ask him questions about what you learned, thank him for what you learned, or ask him what to do next now that you have a better understanding of these topics in Scripture. Also write down any observations or questions that you want to bring to your next group time.

For Next Week: In preparation for next week, read chapter 6 in *How Happiness Happens*.

Session Five

Carry One Another's Burdens

Burdens come in all shapes and sizes. Often, they come as a result of an illness, or a crisis, or a broken relationship. Maybe you've recently felt yourself falling from the resolutions you made to do better, try harder, and walk straighter. Each of us, at one time or another, has spiraled downward—and each of us knows someone who has done the same. It is for this reason that Paul urges, "Carry each other's burdens, and in this way you will fulfill the law of Christ" (Galatians 6:2).

MAX LUCADO

Opening Reflection

The only thing worse than hitting rock bottom is hitting rock bottom *alone*. While "rock bottom" will look different for everyone—yelling at your kids when you promised to stop, making a commitment to a close friend you broke yet again, cheating on a test after resolving to change—we all know what it's like to fall into the pit of sin and wonder if we'll ever get out.

In our individualistic society, we tend to shun relying on one another. If we're suffering, we feel that we have to help ourselves. But this was never the way the Christian faith was intended to be practiced. Our faith is communal in nature. We worship a triune God—Father, Son, Holy Spirit. Jesus ministered with twelve friends by his side. The church was set up to be a body of many members. And it was set up this way for a reason (see 1 Corinthians 12:27).

Paul wrote, "Brothers and sisters, if someone is caught in a sin, you who live by the Spirit should restore that person gently" (Galatians 6:1). This was one way to fulfill the next instruction that Paul gave: "Carry each other's burdens" (verse 2). When we go through life trying to carry every burden, anxiety, sin, and fear alone, we are bound to crumble beneath the weight of the load. But if we are a part of a community that helps carry that load, listens to each other, and pulls people back when they are about to go down the wrong path, we are doing what Paul called "fulfilling the law of Christ" (verse 2).

If you want to guarantee leading a miserable life, then carry your burdens alone. Don't tell anyone about them. Don't ask for help and don't offer to help anyone else. Isolate yourself and see how quickly misery sets in. But if you want joy, peace, and true happiness, you need to share your burdens with others. Let your fellow brothers and sisters in Christ carry your burdens for a while—and offer to carry someone else's.

In this fallen world, you will continue to be tempted by sin and face hardships. But rather than going it alone, realize that you have the body of Christ beside you.

Talk About It

Begin your group time by inviting anyone to share his or her insights from last week's personal study. Next, to get things started, discuss one of the following questions:

- How do you feel about asking for help? Are you quick to ask others for help? Hesitant? Resistant? Why?

—*or*—

- When was the last time someone helped you to carry a burden? What was the burden? How did that person help you?

Hearing the Word

Invite someone to read aloud James 5:16–18. Listen for fresh insights as you hear the verses being read, and then discuss the questions that follow.

> [16] Confess your sins to each other and pray for each other so that you may be healed. The earnest prayer of a righteous person has great power and produces wonderful results. [17] Elijah was as human as we are, and yet when he prayed earnestly that no rain would fall, none fell for three and a half years! [18] Then, when he prayed again, the sky sent down rain and the earth began to yield its crops (NLT).

What is one key insight that stands out to you from this passage?

In what ways did that represent a new insight?

Do you believe your prayers can have the same results as they did for Elijah? Why or why not?

Video Teaching Notes

Play the video segment for session five. As you watch, use the following outline to record any thoughts or concepts that stand out to you.

Carrying one another's burdens is like breaking out your walking stick, hiking alongside a friend, and helping her navigate the rocks, tree roots, and other hazards that could trip her up.

Each of us, at one time or another, has spiraled downward— and each of us knows someone who has done the same. It is for this reason that the apostle Paul urges us to "carry each other's burdens."

This is the law of Christ: *to love one another.* And one way we demonstrate that love is by carrying one another's burdens.

Paul recognized that sin not only infects the believer but also affects the community.

When you engage in prayer, it allows you to shift the burden you are carrying for others onto the shoulders of God.

We have to be willing to do something when we see others struggling under the weight of their burdens. We have to be willing to step out and step up.

If you see a congregation called the "Honking Geese Christian Fellowship," step right in and get acquainted. Geese make community health a priority.

All of us lose our way at times. And when we think back on those times, we will be thankful for the people in our lives who helped us make our way back to the trail.

Rex has had so many challenges. He has been through so much. He has so few of even his mementos that he treasured from the past. At one point, I just said, "Rex, I'm so sorry for all that has happened and for all you've lost." And he said, "Well, I'm not sorry, because I found God." I was stunned by his statement. He's lost his former life . . . but he realizes what he's found. Today, I am so thankful to God for the relationship I have with Rex. His being willing to share with me has made me realize I should be more open to sharing. His kindness is such an example to me. It just means the world to me. I feel the Lord brought Rex into my life instead of bringing me into Rex's life. God has blessed me with Rex's friendship and kindness.

SHARON, FROM THE VIDEO

Group Discussion

Take a few minutes with your group members to discuss what you just watched and explore these concepts in Scripture.

1. Read Galatians 6:2. Has anyone ever carried a burden for you? If so, how did this affect you and the circumstances around that burden?

2. Have you ever witnessed a community coming alongside an individual and carrying that person's burden? What did you think about this act of kindness?

3. Sometimes the burdens that we experience are outside our control—an illness, crisis, broken relationship—and sometimes those burdens are due to our own sin. How can our sin be a burden to us? How can our sin affect those around us?

4. Read Galatians 6:1. What are your thoughts about this instruction from Paul? Does it seem extreme, necessary, helpful? Why do you think Paul suggests the community intervene when an individual is sinning?

5. Think back to the discussion in this week's teaching about the difference between seagulls and geese. How have you witnessed the church acting like geese? Like seagulls? How did these experiences affect the way you view God, Jesus, and the church?

6. How often do you pray for people you know who are facing a difficult sin struggle? Is prayer your first response or last resort? Explain.

7. Is there a Rex in your life—someone who could use help shouldering a burden? Who is that person? How could you pray for that person this week?

8. What is a burden you are carrying right now that you don't want to carry alone anymore? Who is someone you could ask for help?

Closing Activity

To apply today's study, complete the Scripture exercise below:

- *Fill in the blank with your name:* "As for _____, [I was] dead in [my] transgressions and sins, in which [I] used to live when [I] followed the ways of this world and of the ruler of the kingdom of the air" (Ephesians 2:1–2).

- *Fill in the blank with the name of someone who needs to experience the love of Christ:* "For God so loved _____ that he gave his one and only Son, that whoever believes in him shall not perish but have eternal life" (John 3:16).

- *Fill in the blank with the name of someone who needs to experience the restoration of Christ:* "The Lord is not slow in keeping his promise, as some understand slowness. Instead he is patient with _____, not wanting anyone to perish, but everyone to come to repentance" (2 Peter 3:9).

If you feel comfortable, share with your group what this experience was like for you.

Closing Prayer

Break up into groups of two. Take turns praying for one another's burdens—whether those are your own sin burdens or something else that you are carrying. After praying for each other, take turns praying for someone you know outside the group who is facing a sin struggle and could use some help in carrying that burden.

Between-Sessions
Personal Study

Session Five

Reflect on the material you've covered this week in *How Happiness Happens* by engaging in any or all of the following between-sessions activities. Each personal study consists of four days of reflection activities to help you implement what you learned in the group time. The time you invest will be well spent, so let God use it to draw you closer to him. At your next meeting, share any key points or insights that stood out to you as you spent this time with the Lord.

Being Geese in a World of Seagulls

During this week's session, you learned how seagulls differ from geese. Seagulls are self-centered, while geese prioritize community. Seagulls operate with an "every man for himself" mentality, while geese fly together and rotate who leads the flock. Seagulls fight one another for food, while geese will follow a weak bird to the ground and stay with it until it is strong again. Seagulls are jealous of one another, while geese support one another—even honking at each other as a way to encourage the weaker birds.

1. When and where in your life have you experienced a seagull-like culture? How did this environment affect you?

2. When and where in your life have you experienced a geese-like culture? How did this environment affect you?

3. Do you think our society tends to value a seagull lifestyle or a geese lifestyle? Why?

4. Which birds do you think are happier—seagulls or geese? Why?

5. Read the following passages about the church—the body of Christ:

   As iron sharpens iron, so one person sharpens another (Proverbs 27:17).

For just as each of us has one body with many members, and these members do not all have the same function, so in Christ we, though many, form one body (Romans 12:4–5).

And let us consider how we may spur one another on toward love and good deeds, not giving up meeting together, as some are in the habit of doing, but encouraging one another—and all the more as you see the Day approaching (Hebrews 10:24–25).

How does iron sharpening iron represent community (see Proverbs 27:17)? How does a human body represent community (see Romans 12:4–5)?

6. What did the author of Hebrews advise the believers to keep doing (see Hebrews 10:24–25)? Why do you think he gave this particular command?

7. Paul writes, "Carry each other's burdens, and in this way you will fulfill the law of Christ" (Galatians 6:2). What is the "law of Christ" (see John 13:34)? How can carrying one another's burdens fulfill this law?

8. Why do you think God set up faith to be communal rather than individual?

9. Do you feel like you have good community in your life? If so, who are those people? How do they encourage you? How do they help carry your burdens?

10. If you are lacking community, where in your life could you use it most? What do you think is preventing you from finding good community?

Prayer: *Your communal faith mirrors a God who communes with the Trinity—the Father, Son, and Holy Spirit. Today, thank God for his creation—for giving you friends, family, and the church to lean on during hard times. Ask God to bring you community where you need it most. Thank Jesus for carrying the ultimate burden—your sin. Thank him for the cross. Ask him to make you more like him. Finally, ask the Holy Spirit to comfort you and to guide you to community when you feel alone. Ask for courage to reach out when you need help. Also ask for your eyes to be opened to someone in your community who may need your help.*

Reluctance to Engage

Often, we may hold ourselves back from engaging in community because we assume our sin or our problems are too great to share with others. We might even think our sin is too big for God. But the truth is that no sin was left uncleansed by Jesus' sacrifice on the cross, and when we are honest about our sin, the shame lessens. As Paul wrote, "Everything exposed by the light becomes visible—and everything that is illuminated becomes a light" (Ephesians 5:13).

1. What is a current sin struggle in your life? Have you shared this with anyone? Why or why not?

2. Has anyone shared his or her own sin struggle with you? How did it make you feel about that person? How did their sharing affect your relationship with him or her?

3. In Luke 15:1–10, Jesus tells the following parables of the lost sheep and the lost coin:

   [1] The tax collectors and sinners all came to listen to Jesus. [2] But the Pharisees and the teachers of the law

began to complain: "Look, this man welcomes sinners and even eats with them."

[3] Then Jesus told them this story: [4] "Suppose one of you has a hundred sheep but loses one of them. Then he will leave the other ninety-nine sheep in the open field and go out and look for the lost sheep until he finds it. [5] And when he finds it, he happily puts it on his shoulders [6] and goes home. He calls to his friends and neighbors and says, 'Be happy with me because I found my lost sheep.' [7] In the same way, I tell you there is more joy in heaven over one sinner who changes his heart and life, than over ninety-nine good people who don't need to change.

[8] "Suppose a woman has ten silver coins, but loses one. She will light a lamp, sweep the house, and look carefully for the coin until she finds it. [9] And when she finds it, she will call her friends and neighbors and say, 'Be happy with me because I have found the coin that I lost.' [10] In the same way, there is joy in the presence of the angels of God when one sinner changes his heart and life" (NCV).

What caused the Pharisees and the teachers of the law to complain (see verse 2)? Why do you think Jesus responded to their complaint with these parables?

4. In the parable of the lost sheep, what does it say about the shepherd that he would go after just one missing sheep?

5. How does the shepherd react after finding the lost sheep? To what does Jesus compare the shepherd's reaction?

6. In the parable of the lost coin, how does the woman react after finding the coin?

7. Have you ever lost something valuable and then found it? What did you lose? How did you feel when you found it?

8. What truths do these parables reveal about God—who he is and how he feels about us?

9. After reading these parables, how do you think God feels about your struggles with sin?

10. What will you do this week to engage with others and share your burdens with them?

Prayer: *Practice confession during your prayer time today. Admit your sin to God. Ask him for forgiveness. Thank him for sending his Son, Jesus, to forgive all your sins once and for all.*

The Power of Prayer

At times, we can feel intimidated by the problems that other people bring to us. However, we need to remember God does not call us to *fix* each other's problems or make one another's burdens *disappear*. God knows we, as humans, are not capable of doing so. He simply asks that we help shoulder the load. Prayer is one way we accomplish this task.

1. What role does prayer play in your life? What role would you like it to play in your life?

2. Do you believe in the power of prayer? Why or why not?

3. Review again what James writes to the believers concerning the power of prayer:

> [16] Confess your sins to each other and pray for each other so that you may be healed. The earnest prayer of a righteous person has great power and produces wonderful results. [17] Elijah was as human as we are, and yet when he prayed earnestly that no rain would fall, none fell for three and a half years! [18] Then, when he prayed again, the sky sent down rain and the earth began to yield its crops (James 5:16–18 NLT).

What does James say in this passage will happen when we confess our sins to each other and pray for one another?

4. What does James say about the power of a righteous person's prayers?

5. James references Elijah, an Old Testament prophet who declared there would be a famine in the land of Israel until he called for rain. Three and a half years later, Elijah

prayed to God to send that rain. Read the following portion of the story from 1 Kings 18:41–46:

[41] Then Elijah said to Ahab, "Now, go, eat, and drink, because a heavy rain is coming." [42] So King Ahab went to eat and drink. At the same time Elijah climbed to the top of Mount Carmel, where he bent down to the ground with his head between his knees.

[43] Then Elijah said to his servant, "Go and look toward the sea."

The servant went and looked. "I see nothing," he said.

Elijah told him to go and look again. This happened seven times. [44] The seventh time, the servant said, "I see a small cloud, the size of a human fist, coming from the sea."

Elijah told the servant, "Go to Ahab and tell him to get his chariot ready and go home now. Otherwise, the rain will stop him."

[45] After a short time the sky was covered with dark clouds. The wind began to blow, and soon a heavy rain began to fall. Ahab got in his chariot and started back to Jezreel. [46] The LORD gave his power to Elijah (NCV).

What does Elijah tell King Ahab at the beginning of this passage (see verse 41)?

6. Why do you think that Elijah makes this statement to the king before he prays for rain? What does this say about Elijah's faith?

7. How many times does Elijah tell his servant to go check the sky for signs of rain? What does this tell you about Elijah's faith?

8. "The LORD gave his power to Elijah" (verse 46). Do you believe God has given you this same kind of power in prayer? Why or why not?

9. It might be tempting to believe Elijah's prayer was heard because he was a great prophet. But Jesus says, "Truly I tell you, if you have faith as small as a mustard seed, you can say to this mountain, 'Move from here to there,' and it will move. Nothing will be impossible for you" (Matthew 17:20). What size is your faith when it comes to prayer? Is it big like Elijah's or small like a mustard seed?

10. What is something for which you need prayer? What is something for which a person in your life needs prayer?

Prayer: *Today, pray boldly for the things that you identified during this exercise. Ask God to provide exactly what you need or what another person in your life needs. Ask God to give you faith as you pray this prayer to him, and be honest with the Lord about your doubts. Spend a few moments in silence listening for God's voice.*

Further Reflection

Reflect on what you studied this week: your community in Christ, the importance of being honest about sin, and the power of prayer. Journal your thoughts or write them as a prayer to God, whether you need to ask him questions about what you learned, thank him for what you learned, or ask him what to do next now that you have a better understanding of these topics in Scripture. Also write down any observations or questions that you want to bring to your next group time.

For Next Week: In preparation for next week, read chapters 9 and 11 in *How Happiness Happens*.

Session Six

Love One Another

The New Testament contains fifty-nine "one another" statements that show us how to make happiness happen in our lives. But one of these commands appears far more times than the rest, and it is given not only by Paul, Peter, and John, but also by Jesus himself. It is the greatest of all the "one another" commands—and sowing even one act of it can produce an unexpected and abundant harvest of joy. What is this command? Simply this: "Love one another" (1 John 3:11).

M A X   L U C A D O

Opening Reflection

Each of the "one another" passages we have studied so far in this series—accept one another, bear with one another, serve one another, forgive one another, and carry one another's burdens—could fall under the umbrella of the ultimate "one another" passage we will study this week. This particular "one another" instruction is given multiple times in the New Testament and is best expressed by Jesus himself: "A new command I give you: Love one another. As I have loved you, so you must love one another" (John 13:34).

The type of love Jesus talks about in this verse isn't in word only. It is not simply saying, "I love my neighbor." The love Jesus refers to in this passage is a *transformational* kind of love—a love that makes us want to be better people and brings out the best in us. Perhaps you have experienced this type of love. A spouse, friend, or family member made you want to be a better *you* or made you realize that you were capable of more than you imagined. If so, you have experienced the love of Christ through another person.

Jesus' love for you has changed you. His death, burial, and resurrection have brought you the possibility of new life. When you accept his offer of salvation, your identity changes from sinner to saved, from banished to welcome into his kingdom, from orphan to beloved child of God. His love is life-changing—and once you've experienced that love for yourself, you can then love others in a way that reflects Christ.

Of course, loving one another is often easier said than done. People can be difficult—even the ones we love the most—and we can grow weary of them. It's easy to run out of love for the people who exhaust us, anger us, and begrudge us. But as we read in 1 John 4:19, "We love because he first loved us." God's love for us through Jesus is endless. We will never run out of it. We will always be loved. Because of this, we can always love others.

Can you imagine a world in which everyone loved as Christ loved? We would all be our best selves, filled with confidence, hope, humility, and peace. Can you imagine how happy that world would be?

Talk About It

Begin your group time by inviting anyone to share his or her insights from last week's personal study. Next, to get things started, discuss one of the following questions:

- Which of the "one another" statements that we have studied in this series has been the most challenging for you? Why?

—or—

- What comes to mind when you think about the command to love one another? What does it look like to love the people in your world?

Hearing the Word

Invite someone to read aloud Ephesians 3:17–19. Listen for fresh insights as you hear the verses being read, and then discuss the questions that follow.

> [17] And I pray that you, being rooted and established in love, [18] may have power, together with all the Lord's holy people, to grasp how wide and long and high and deep is the love of Christ, [19] and to know this love that surpasses knowledge—that you may be filled to the measure of all the fullness of God.

What is one key insight that stands out to you from this passage?

In what ways did that represent a new insight?

Do you feel like you grasp how wide, long, high, and deep the love of Christ is? Why or why not?

Video Teaching Notes

Play the video segment for session six. As you watch, use the following outline to record any thoughts or concepts that stand out to you.

Sowing even one small act of love can produce an abundant harvest of joy . . . for ourselves and the other person.

Agape love writes the check when the balance is low. It forgives the mistake when the offense is high. It offers patience when stress is abundant. It extends kindness when kindness is rare.

We don't love people because people are lovable. We love others because we have come to experience and believe the love that God has for us.

We would think *agape* love has limits. Surely there has to be an end to it somewhere! But David the adulterer never found it. Paul the murderer never found it. Peter the liar never found it. When it came to life, they hit bottom. But when it came to God's love, they never did.

Agape love finds beauty in the collage of humanity. Apart from each other, we are just brushstrokes on a canvas. But together, we are God's workmanship.

Admonishment is high-octane encouragement. It is to deposit truth into a person's thoughts. It is to refuse to sit idly by while the enemy spreads his lies. It is done out of love.

You have a tool chest at your disposal—encouragements, admonitions, warm greetings, words of prayer. Restore your relationships with patience, kindness, and unselfishness. Do whatever it takes to bring out the best in others.

Today, be the person whom people are glad to see and the voice that people want to hear. Drive the "happiness truck." In the end, you'll see that you are the one smiling the most.

Group Discussion

Take a few minutes with your group members to discuss what
you just watched and explore these concepts in Scripture.

1. Think of the metaphor of the art conservator restoring
   an old painting to its former shine and brilliance. How
   does this represent the way believers in Christ help others
   to "shine" by loving one another?

---

*I lived for sixty-eight years being a person of independence
and in charge. But in 2017, the doctor told me I had ALS. The
biggest concern was the loss of voice, so I was directed to do
voice banking. It was a daunting challenge. There are nearly
2,000 phrases you have to repeat, and they're nonsensical
phrases, so you really are at the mercy of the program. Ste-
phen not only had the compassion and kindness I needed,
but he also had the expertise to understand how to accomplish the task. The actual accomplishment of doing the
program took approximately two months, and I learned a lot
of lessons in the process. One was that it's always been
easier for me to give love than to receive it. I was put in a
position where I had to receive—and this taught me how
amazing it is just to lean back and receive love and support.*

LINDA, FROM THE VIDEO

---

2. Read Matthew 22:34–40. How does Jesus say we are to love God? Why is the command to "love one another" truly the greatest "one another" passage in Scripture?

3. Read 1 Corinthians 13:4–8. Based on this passage, how would you define *agape* love? How does it differ from romantic love? From love for your fellow humans?

4. Read Romans 15:14. How would you define *admonishment*? How can admonishing someone show that person the love of Christ?

5. Has anyone ever admonished you? How did that type of encouragement affect you?

6. Who are some of the people in your life who bring out the best in you? How do they do this? How do you feel after spending time with them?

7. Linda confessed in her testimony that it is hard for her to let others love her. Have you ever struggled with letting others love you? If so, why do you think that is?

8. Accepting the love of Christ can be just as difficult as accepting love from others. Do you feel like you have accepted the love of Jesus? Why or why not?

Closing Activity

To help apply today's study, break up into pairs and speak the following passages over each other. (Note: If you have an odd number of people in your group, one of the pairs can take on an additional member.) Insert your partner's name where you see a blank to make it more personal:

- For God has not given _____ a spirit of fear, but of power and of love and of a sound mind (2 Timothy 1:7 NKJV).

- I pray that you, _____, being rooted and established in love, may have power, together with all the Lord's holy people, to grasp how wide and long and high and deep is the love of Christ, and to know this love that surpasses knowledge—that you may be filled to the measure of all the fullness of God (Ephesians 3:17–19).

- [Jesus'] grace is sufficient for you, _____ _____, for [his] power is made perfect in weakness (2 Corinthians 12:9).

After you have finished, talk about which admonishment resonated with you the most.

Closing Prayer

Close your time by spending time with your heavenly Father. Using the prompts below, have one person lead your group in a time of prayer:

- Thank God for the time you have shared together during the past six weeks, and thank him that you have discovered (or rediscovered) where true happiness comes from.
- Confess that you don't always look for happiness in the right places and that you need to learn these lessons again and again.
- Ask God to help you grasp the love of Christ and what it means for you—and that he would help you love others with an *agape* type of love.
- Praise God for sending his Son, Jesus, so you would always know your heavenly Father loves you, cares for you, and is watching over you.

Between-Sessions
Personal Study

Session Six

Reflect on the material you've covered this week in *How Happiness Happens* by engaging in any or all of the following activities. Each personal study consists of four days of reflection activities to help you implement what you learned in the group time. The time you invest will be well spent, so let God use it to draw you closer to him. Be sure to share with your group leader or group members in the upcoming weeks any key points or insights that stood out to you.

Agape Love

Jesus said, "A new command I give you: Love one another. As I have loved you, so you must love one another" (John 13:34). As we have seen, the Greek word for *love* in this passage is *agape*, which means to welcome, dearly love, be fond of, and be well pleased with.[12] This is the kind of love that "writes the check when the balance is low . . . forgives the mistake when the offense is high . . . offers patience when stress is abundant . . . extends kindness when kindness is rare."

1. Before this study, how did you define love? Where did you learn that definition?

2. John uses the word *agape* twenty-seven times in his Gospel, which is more than any other book in the New Testament. (The letter of 1 John comes in second, with seventeen uses of the word.) Read the following verses, in which John uses the word *agape* to help explain the love of God and the love of Christ:

For God so loved the world that he gave his one and only Son, that whoever believes in him shall not perish but have eternal life (John 3:16).

The Father loves the Son and has placed everything in his hands (John 3:35).

The reason my Father loves me is that I lay down my life—only to take it up again. No one takes it from me, but I lay it down of my own accord. I have authority to lay it down and authority to take it up again. This command I received from my Father (John 10:17–18).

How did God show his love for you (see John 3:16)? What does that say about God?

3. What promise are you given for believing in Christ? What does this mean for you?

4. How can you know that God loves Jesus (see John 3:35)? Do you ever think about God loving Jesus? Why is it important for you to know how God feels about his Son?

5. Why does God love Jesus (see John 10:17–18)? What does this say about the type of love God values? What does this say about the nature of the love of Christ?

6. In the past, when you heard the phrase "God loves you," what did this mean to you? In light of the verses above, how would you describe God's love for you?

7. John also uses the word *agape* to show how we are to love God and others:

Because of the Pharisees they would not openly acknowledge their faith for fear they would be put out of the synagogue; for they loved human praise more than praise from God (John 12:42–43).

Anyone who loves me will obey my teaching. My Father will love them, and we will come to them and make our home with them. Anyone who does not love me will not obey my teaching (John 14:23–24).

Just as the Father has loved Me, I have also loved you; abide in My love (John 15:9 NASB).

John addresses an important topic in 12:42–43: our human tendency to love the praise of people more than the praise of God. When do you find that you crave the love of others more than the love of God? Why did Jesus warn against this?

8. How can you show your love for Jesus (see John 14:23–24)? What do these verses tell you about *agape* love?

9. What does it mean to *abide* in Jesus' love (see John 15:9)?

10. What are some practical ways you could abide in Jesus' love this week?

Prayer: *In your prayer time today, abide in the love of Christ. Think about how he showed his great love for you. Think about what you must mean to Jesus for him to willingly lay down his life for you. Ask him to help you abide in his love as you move throughout your day. End your time by sitting still in silence and listening for the loving voice of God. What is he telling you?*

Admonishing One Another

In Romans 15:14, Paul wrote, "Now I myself am confident concerning you, my brethren, that you also are full of goodness, filled with all knowledge, able also to admonish one another" (NKJV). Admonishing is one way we can show God's love to one another—but it is more than simple encouragement.

1. Based on this week's teaching, how would you define *admonishment*?

2. Have you ever felt admonished by someone else? What did that person say or do to admonish you? How did it make you feel?

3. We can admonish others by speaking truth over them. However, while the truth is always encouraging to our spirits, it can sometimes be hard for us to hear. In Matthew 16:21–23, we read how Jesus had to speak some hard truths to Peter:

> 21 From that time Jesus began to show to His disciples that He must go to Jerusalem, and suffer many things from the elders and chief priests and scribes, and be killed, and be raised the third day.
> 22 Then Peter took Him aside and began to rebuke Him, saying, "Far be it from You, Lord; this shall not happen to You!"
> 23 But He turned and said to Peter, "Get behind Me, Satan! You are an offense to Me, for you are not mindful of the things of God, but the things of men" (NKJV).

What prompted Peter to take Jesus aside and begin to rebuke him?

4. How did Jesus admonish Peter for this outburst? Why did Jesus do this?

5. How would you feel if Jesus corrected you in this way?

6. This exchange occurred right after another conversation between Peter and Jesus that you studied in a previous session. In Matthew 16:17–19, Jesus said to Peter:

> [17] Blessed are you, Simon Bar-Jonah, for flesh and blood has not revealed this to you, but My Father who is in heaven. [18] And I also say to you that you are Peter, and on this rock I will build My church, and the gates of Hades shall not prevail against it. [19] And I will give you the keys of the kingdom of heaven, and whatever you bind on earth will be bound in heaven, and whatever you loose on earth will be loosed in heaven (NKJV).

How is this different from what Jesus said to Peter in Matthew 16:23?

7. Based on these conversations, how do you think Jesus felt about Peter? How do you think Peter felt about Jesus?

8. Again, remember that these conversations appear side by side in Scripture. What does this tell you about how we are to admonish one another?

9. Is there anyone in your life whom you trust to give you both words of encouragement and words of admonishment or correction? Who is that person?

10. Why do you trust the person? Who in your life trusts you to give words of admonishment in the same manner?

Prayer: *As you end your time in prayer, use the questions below to act as a guide in your conversation with God. Spend a few moments in silence as you consider each one:*

- *Has anyone spoken truth into your life recently—something encouraging that you may have dismissed in the moment but need to remember now?*

- *Has anyone spoken a difficult truth into your life recently—something that may have been hurtful but was also truthful?*
- *If so, how could you receive that truth today?*
- *Is there anyone in your life whom God is calling you to admonish?*
- *If so, what do you sense that God wants you to say to this person?*
- *Do you sense any admonishment in your life from the Holy Spirit today?*

Spend some time listening for God's words of truth, encouragement, or correction in love.

Accepting God's Love

It is important to accept yourself in order to accept others, and it also is important to forgive yourself in order to forgive others. But accepting and forgiving yourself are only possible by accepting the love of Christ. When you have accepted that Jesus loves you, you are then able to follow Jesus' command: "As I have loved you, so you must love one another" (John 13:34).

1. Do you believe that Jesus loves you? Why or why not?

2. God's greatest demonstration of love for us was through Jesus' death on the cross. Paul writes, "I have been crucified

with Christ and I no longer live, but Christ lives in me. The life I now live in the body, I live by faith in the Son of God, who loved me and gave himself for me" (Galatians 2:20). What does it mean to be "crucified" with Christ?

3. What did Paul recognize about God's love for him?

4. Consider the following passages about the depth of God's love for you:

Your love, LORD, reaches to the heavens, your faithfulness to the skies. Your righteousness is like the highest mountains, your justice like the great deep. You, LORD, preserve both people and animals. How priceless is your unfailing love, O God! People take refuge in the shadow of your wings (Psalm 36:5–7).

For I am convinced that neither death nor life, neither angels nor demons, neither the present nor the future, nor any powers, neither height nor depth, nor anything else in all creation, will be able to separate us from the love of God that is in Christ Jesus our Lord (Romans 8:38–39).

I pray that you, being rooted and established in love, may have power, together with all the Lord's holy people, to grasp how wide and long and high and deep is the love of Christ, and to know this love that surpasses knowledge—that you may be filled to the measure of all the fullness of God (Ephesians 3:17–19).

How did David describe God's love (see Psalm 36:5–7)? If God's love is so vast, why can it still be hard to believe that he truly loves you?

5. What things can never separate us from the love of God (see Romans 8:38–39)?

6. Do you feel anything is separating you from the love of God? If so, what?

7. In light of Romans 8:38–39, do you think this thing—whether it is sin, your past, your unbelief—can really keep you apart from God? Why or why not?

8. What does Paul say will happen if we are rooted and established in Christ's love (see Ephesians 3:17–19)?

9. How has *not* accepting God's love prevented you from loving others? How could accepting the love of Christ on a daily basis help you love those around you more?

10. Think of someone in your life who is difficult to love. Considering the passages you read today, how does God want you to love this person?

Prayer: *Speak honestly with God today. If anything is holding you back from accepting his full love for you, tell him what it is. Ask him to help you accept his love. Ask him to help you believe in it. Thank him* *for showing you his love by sending his Son to die for you, and ask for a renewed sense of awe at this great act. Walk away from today's study confident that you are loved by the Creator of the universe.*

Further Reflection

Reflect on what you studied this week: *agape* love, admonishing others, and accepting the love of Christ. Journal your thoughts or write them as a prayer to God, whether you need to ask him questions about what you learned, thank him for what you learned, or ask him what to do next now that you have a better understanding of these topics in Scripture.

Leader's Guide

Thank you for your willingness to lead a group through *How Happiness Happens*! What you have chosen to do is important, and much good fruit can come from studies like this. The rewards of being a leader are different from those of participating, and we hope that as you lead you will find your own walk with Jesus deepened by this experience.

How Happiness Happens is a six-session study built around video content and small-group interaction. As the group leader, imagine yourself as the host of a dinner party. Your job is to take care of your guests by managing all the behind-the-scenes details so that as your guests arrive, they can focus on each other and on interaction around the topic.

As the group leader, your role is not to answer all the questions or reteach the content—the video, book, and study guide will do most of that work. Your job is to guide the experience and cultivate your small group into a kind of teaching community. This will make it a place for members to process, question, and reflect—not receive more instruction.

There are several elements in this leader's guide that will help you as you structure your study and reflection time, so follow along and take advantage of each one.

Before You Begin

Before your first meeting, make sure the group members have a copy of this study guide so they can follow along and have their answers written out ahead of time. Alternately, you can hand out the study guides at your first meeting and give the group members some time to look over the material and ask any preliminary questions. During your first meeting, be sure to send a blank sheet of paper around the room and have members write down their name, phone number, and email address so you can keep in touch with them during the week.

Generally, the ideal size for a group is between eight to ten people, which will ensure that everyone will have enough time to participate in discussions. If you have more people, you might want to break up the main group into smaller subgroups. Encourage those who show up at the first meeting to commit to attending the duration of the study, as this will help the group members get to know each other, create stability for the group, and help you know how to prepare each week.

Each of the sessions begins with an opening reflection. The two questions that follow in the "Talk About It" section serve as an icebreaker to get the group members thinking about the topic at hand. Some people may want to tell a long story in response to one of these questions, but the goal is to keep the answers brief. Ideally, you want everyone in the group to get a chance to answer, so try to keep the responses to a minute or less. If you have talkative group members, say up front that everyone needs to limit the answer to one minute.

Give the group members a chance to answer, but tell them to feel free to pass if they wish. With the rest of the study, it's generally not a good idea to have everyone answer every question—a free-flowing discussion is more desirable. But with the opening icebreaker question, you can go around the circle. Encourage shy people to share, but don't force them.

Before your first meeting, let the group members know that each session contains four between-sessions activities that they can complete during the week. While this is an optional exercise, it will help the members cement the concepts presented during the group study time and encourage them to spend time each day in God's Word. Also invite them to bring any questions and insights they uncovered during their study to your next meeting, especially if they had a breakthrough moment or didn't understand something.

Weekly Preparation

As the leader, there are a few things you should do to prepare for each meeting:

- *Read through the session.* This will help you to become familiar with the content and know how to structure the discussion times.
- *Decide which questions you want to discuss.* Based on the amount and length of group discussion, you may not be able to get through all of the Bible study and group discussion questions, so choose four to five questions that you definitely want to cover.
- *Be familiar with the questions you want to discuss.* When the group meets you'll be watching the clock, so be familiar with the questions you have selected. In this way, you'll ensure you have the material more deeply in your mind than your group members.

- *Pray for your group.* Pray for your group members throughout the week and ask God to lead them as they study his Word.

Note that in many cases there will be no one "right" answer to a question. Answers will vary, especially when the group members are being asked to share their personal experiences.

Structuring the Discussion Time

Determine with your group how long you want to meet each week so you can plan your time accordingly. Generally, most groups like to meet for either sixty minutes or ninety minutes, so you could use one of the following schedules:

SECTION	60 MIN.	90 MIN.
WELCOME (members arrive)	5 min.	10 min.
ICEBREAKER (discuss one of the two opening questions for the session)	10 min.	10 min.
SCRIPTURE (read the opening passage and answer the questions)	5 min.	10 min.
VIDEO (watch the teaching material together and take notes)	15 min.	15 min.
DISCUSSION (discuss the Bible study questions you selected ahead of time)	20 min.	35 min.
PRAYER/CLOSING (pray together as a group and dismiss)	5 min.	10 min.

As the group leader, it is up to you to keep track of the time and keep things moving along according to your schedule. You might want to set a timer for each segment so both you and the group members know when your time is up. (Note that there are some good phone apps for timers that play a gentle chime or other pleasant sound instead of a disruptive noise.)

Don't be concerned if the group members are quiet or slow to share. People are often quiet when they are pulling together their ideas, and this might be a new experience for them. Just ask a question and let it hang in the air until someone shares. You can then say, "Thank you. What about others? What came to you when you watched that portion of the video?"

Group Dynamics

Leading a group through the *How Happiness Happens* study will prove to be highly rewarding for both you and your group members. However, this doesn't mean you will not encounter any challenges along the way! Discussions can get off track. Group members may not be sensitive to the needs and ideas of others. Some might worry they will be expected to talk about matters that make them feel awkward. Others may express comments that result in disagreements. To help ease this strain on you and the group, consider establishing the following ground rules for your group:

* When someone raises a question or comment that is off the main topic, suggest you deal with it another time, or, if you feel led to go in that

direction, let the group know you will be spending some time discussing it.

- If someone asks a question you don't know how to answer, admit it and move on. At your discretion, feel free to invite group members to comment on questions that call for personal experience.

- If you find one or two people are dominating the discussion time, direct a few questions to others in the group. Outside the main group time, ask the more dominating members to help you draw out the quieter ones. Work to make them a part of the solution instead of the problem.

- When a disagreement occurs, encourage the group members to process the matter in love. Encourage those on opposite sides to restate what they heard the other side say about the matter, and then invite each side to evaluate if that perception is accurate. Lead the group in examining other Scriptures related to the topic and look for common ground.

When any of these issues arise, encourage your group members to follow these words from the Bible: "Love one another" (John 13:34), "If it is possible, as far as it depends on you, live at peace with everyone" (Romans 12:18), and "Be quick to listen, slow to speak and slow to become angry" (James 1:19). This will make your group time more rewarding and beneficial for everyone who attends.

Thank you again for your willingness to lead your group. May God reward your efforts and make your time together in *How Happiness Happens* fruitful for his kingdom.

Endnotes

1. Kathy Caprino, "The Top 10 Things People Want in Life but Can't Seem to Get," *Huffington Post*, December 6, 2017, https://www.huffingtonpost.com/kathy-caprino/the-top-10-things-people-_2_b_9564982.html.

2. David Shimer, "Yale's Most Popular Class Ever: Happiness," *New York Times*, January 26, 2018, https://www.nytimes.com/2018/01/26/nyregion/at-yale-class-on-happiness-draws-huge-crowd-laurie-santos.html.

3. Alexandra Sifferlin, *"Here's How Happy Americans Are Right Now,"* TIME, July 26, 2017, http://time.com/4871720/how-happy-are-americans/.

4. Tremper Longman III and David E. Garland, eds., *The Expositor's Bible Commentary: Luke–Acts* (Grand Rapids, MI: Zondervan, 2007), vol. 10, notes on Luke 5:27, 15:1, and 19:2.

5. Edwin A. Blum and Jeremy Royal Howard, eds., *Holman Christian Standard Study Bible* (Nashville, TN: Holman Bible Publishers, 2010), p. 1811.

6. W. E. Vine, *Vine's Expository Dictionary of New Testament Words: A Comprehensive Dictionary of the Original Greek Words with Their Precise Meanings for English Readers* (McLean, VA: MacDonald Publishing, n.d.), "Longsuffering," p. 694.

7. Joseph Thayer and William Smith, "Greek Lexicon Entry for *Makrothumia*," in *The New American Standard New Testament*

Greek Lexicon, https://www.biblestudytools.com/lexicons/greek/nas/makrothumia.html.

8. Ibid., "Greek Lexicon Entry for *Paraklesis*," https://www.bible studytools.com/lexicons/greek/nas/paraklesis.html.

9. Craig S. Keener, *The IVP Bible Background Commentary: New Testament* (Downers Grove, IL: InterVarsity Press, 1993), p. 297.

10. Ibid., p. 95.

11. Ibid., p. 96.

12. James Strong, *Strong's Exhaustive Concordance of the Bible*, Greek #25, https://www.biblestudytools.com/lexicons/greek/nas/agapao.html.

ALSO AVAILABLE
FROM MAX LUCADO

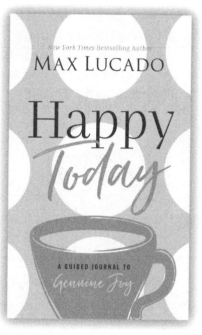

In a world searching for happiness, bestselling author Max Lucado provides a personal plan for a life filled with lasting and fulfilling joy, supported by Jesus' teaching and modern research. *How Happiness Happens* presents a surprising but practical way of living that will change you from the inside out.

In this 52-week guided journal, each week includes an excerpt of Max's writing, a scripture, and a guided journal prompt, alongside journaling space with photos and beautiful illustrations on each spread. This beautiful book is great to work through independently or as you read Max Lucado's *How Happiness Happens*.

More from Max Lucado

Anxiety doesn't have to dominate life. Max looks at seven admonitions from the apostle Paul in Philippians 4:4–8 that lead to one wonderful promise: "The peace of God which surpasses all understanding." He shows how God is ready to give comfort to help us face the calamities in life, view bad news through the lens of sovereignty, discern the lies of Satan, and tell ourselves the truth. We can discover true peace from God that surpasses all human understanding.

Study Guide	DVD	Hardcover
9780310087311	9780310087335	9780718096120

Available now at your favorite bookstore,
or streaming video on StudyGateway.com.